THE LONDON

Covent Garden, Trafalgar Square & the Strand

COVENT GARDEN is once more what it was 250 years ago – the great magnet for London's pleasure seekers. The Piazza has plenty of restaurants, but the surrounding streets and alleys, with their fascinating buildings and rich patina of history, are a feast. With the help of this guide you can steer your way round Seven Dials, discover the secret that lies behind Comyn Ching and find the ancient shop fronts in Goodwin's Court, stroll down to the Adelphi and the Savoy, or up to the handsome yet half-forgotten church of St Giles.

You will meet SAMUEL PEPYS entertaining John Evelyn in Buckingham Street and Benjamin Franklin NAKED in Craven Street, either side of Charing Cross; NELL GWYNN and the ghosts of Drury Lane; BOSWELL watching Garrick and KIPLING watching a suicide; DICKENS on his feverish night walks. You will visit two national galleries, two opera houses, two museums, and London's most EROTIC sculpture, as well as the more staid figures that keep NELSON company in Trafalgar Square.

THE LONDON GUIDES

Covent Garden, Trafalgar Square & the Strand

ROGER HUDSON

Photographs by
JOE WHITLOCK BLUNDELL

HAGGERSTON PRESS

© Text: Roger Hudson, 1996
© Photographs: Joe Whitlock Blundell, 1996

First published in 1996
by The Haggerston Press,
38 Kensington Place, London w8 7PR
Unauthorised duplication contravenes
applicable laws

Printed in Great Britain

A CIP record is available from the British Library

1–869812–13–1

COVER PHOTOS

Front: Trafalgar Square and St Martin-in-the-Fields
Inside front: The Royal Society of Arts, John Adam Street
Inside back: The Warner Cinema, Leicester Square

FRONTISPIECE

John Nash's pepper pots, St Martin's
and the National Gallery

CONTENTS

MAPS

Detailed maps appear on the following pages:

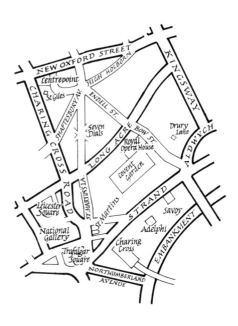

Begin at **Tottenham Court Road Tube** where you should look about you while still underground because it is decorated with the largest scheme of mosaics commissioned in Europe this century, designed by Eduardo Paolozzi, and installed in 1984–5. This Italian-Scot was first famous for his Pop Art collages and something of that technique is detectable here. Spot the Egyptian mummy case alluding to the nearby British Museum, saxophones for the local musical instrument shops, video games and electrical circuits for the computer and hi-fi shops, a fast-food chicken, an urban running man representing the Orwellian commuter. Some are boldly coloured to match the red of the Central Line, others more subdued for the black Northern.

Emerge and walk southwards – down the west side of Charing Cross Road. From here you can crane upwards at the thirty-two floors of **Centrepoint**, that product of the unnatural coupling between the property developers and the planners in the late 1950s and 60s. The planners wanted extra space for ring roads and for roundabouts, and to widen existing roads. The developers had been quietly accumulating property since the end of the War and so had space to sell – at a price. It wasn't money that changed hands, but the right to ignore the normal 'plot ratios', to get much more office space on a site by being allowed to build upwards. Harry Hyams owned the land at St Giles Circus, and his architect, Colonel Richard Seifert, was allowed to raise this overmighty tower in return for a few square yards on which to lay out half a roundabout, soon lost in a one-way system.

The base of the tower is a series of uninviting open staircases, platforms and ramps to underground parking, together with a fountain, which never seems to play, in the middle of an offcut from a municipal swimming pool. Above all this soars the screen

St Giles-in-the-Fields

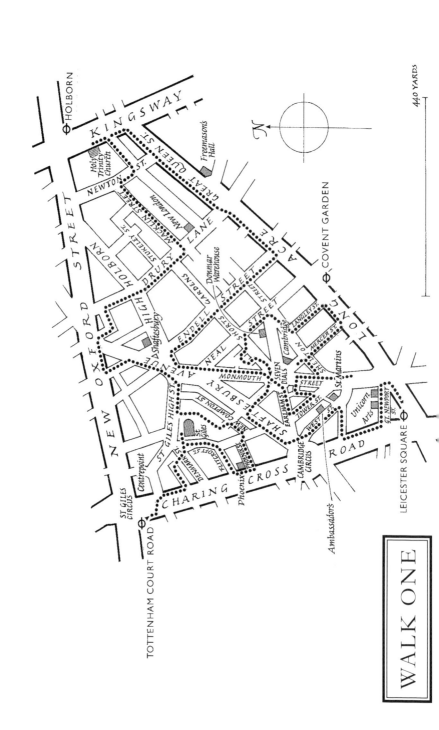

WALK ONE

of angular concrete honeycomb. It remained empty for a number of years, but now houses the Confederation of British Industry, and was listed in 1995 not so much for its architectural qualities but rather as the archetypal example of its kind. Surely future generations could take the mediocrity of the period on trust, without Centrepoint continuing to act as a reminder. Someone pointed out at the time of the listing that it stands on the site of the gallows where **Sir John Oldcastle** was first hanged and then burnt in 1417, but not before he laid a comprehensive curse on the spot. Oldcastle was the original of Shakespeare's character Sir John Falstaff but, while a friend of Henry V, he had not been a drinking companion of him in his youth. In fact Oldcastle was of a puritanical cast of mind, as a leader of the Lollards, the proto-Protestant sect forced underground in the previous century. He was involved in a failed Lollard rising in 1414 and the gallows were located at St Giles because that was where the Lollards from the City were to have joined those from the country. Henry V thwarted them by shutting the City gates.

Cross to the east side of Charing Cross Road a little below the dead fountain and, if you are a connoisseur of alleys, passages and culs-de-sac, go up Denmark Place before turning right at the 12 Bar Club into **Denmark Street**. These are named after Prince George of Denmark, Queen Anne's consort, whom she married in 1683. Much more recently, when it was the centre of the 'light' music industry, Denmark Street was known as Tin Pan Alley. But pop music has floated away from the area on a tide of megabucks, leaving behind some musical instrument shops and some early eighteenth-century houses, such as number 6, occupied by the Zeno Greek Bookshop and painted Greek blue.

It might well have been one of these that housed Marianne Charpillon, her mother and her grandmother when they were living in Denmark Street in 1763. All three were prostitutes when **Giacomo Casanova** first encountered them in Paris in 1759, where they relieved him of 6000 francs and then escaped. When he came to London four years later he was once more ensnared by Marianne, even though at one point he found her in the arms of a barber. When told she was dying, he was determined to commit suicide and loaded himself with lead before setting out for the

A section of Centre-point from St Giles High Street

A typical Denmark Street emporium

Thames. Luckily he met a friend en route who told him the story was a fabrication. He finally brought charges against Marianne's mother and her sisters and they were jailed. Two weeks later Marianne got Casanova bound over to keep the peace before the magistrate Sir John Fielding (p. 50). By this time, his infatuation had cost Casanova a further 2000 guineas. He got some measure of revenge by teaching a parrot to squawk in French, 'the Charpillon is a greater whore than her mother'.

At the eastern end of Denmark Street is **ST GILES-IN-THE-FIELDS**. The church was founded in 1101 by Queen Matilda, wife of Henry I and granddaughter of that King Duncan of Scotland who was murdered by Macbeth. This spot, out in the open countryside well to the west of the City, was chosen because the church was part of a hospital for lepers. The only way society had been able to deal with this contagious disease – the most feared until the coming of the Black Death in the 1340s – was to expel those suffering from it after reading the burial service over them and depriving them of their common legal rights. Thus the hospital of St Giles and another similar one dedicated to St James, from which the present Palace derives, represented a great humanitarian advance. The hospital disappeared at the time of the Dissolution of the Monasteries under Henry VIII but its chapel became the parish church, until pulled down in 1624. Its replacement lasted for about 100 years until the present church was built under the auspices of the local landlord, the Duke of Bedford. He gave the job to the architect on his Bloomsbury estate, Henry Flitcroft. The son of William III's gardener and by training a joiner, Flitcroft fell off some scaffolding while working at the house of the Earl of Burlington in Piccadilly. This happy accident brought him to the attention of the earl, himself an architect of high seriousness dedicated to propagating the ideas of Palladio in Britain. Flitcroft soon became an accomplished draughtsman and acquired the nickname of 'Burlington Harry'. He did not look far for models when designing St Giles, drawing his ideas from Gibbs' St Martin-in-the-Fields and from Wren's St James, Piccadilly.

As so often with London churches, the interior is unexpectedly quiet, the stillness accentuated by the ticking of a clock. Gradually the eye absorbs its overall dignity, propriety and restraint: the dark wood, pale mustard-yellow walls and just the right amount of gilt.

Then one starts to pick out the odd detail – the gilded pelican-in-her-piety at the top of the reredos, the splendid tasselled red velvet cushion on the ledge of the pulpit ready to give off a dramatic cloud of dust when thumped by the preacher to drive home a point. To one side, there is the top layer of a three-decker pulpit from West Street Chapel (p. 28) regularly used by the Wesley brothers in the eighteenth century.

The most famous memorial in the church is to the poet **Andrew Marvell**, who once reminded his coy mistress that

> The grave's a fine and private place,
> But none, I think, do there embrace.

He also asked himself some questions which seem particularly apt under the shadow of Centrepoint:

> Why should, of all things, man unruled
> Such unproportioned dwellings build? ...
> What need of all this marble crust
> T'impark the wanton mote of dust?

The memorial, to 'the ornament and example of his age', was put up by a grand-nephew in 1764, although Marvell had died in 1678. John Aubrey says 'some suspect that he was poysoned by the Jesuits, but I cannot be positive.' In 1692 one Richard Morton gave a more likely explanation, medical incompetence:

... a great febrifuge was given, a draught, that is to say, of Venice treacle, etc. By the doctor's orders, the patient was covered up close with blankets, say rather, was buried under them; and composed himself to sleep and sweat, so that he might escape the cold shivers which are wont to accompany the onset of the ague-fit. He was seized with the deepest sleep and colliquative sweats, and in the short space of twenty-four hours from the time of the ague-fit, he died comatose. He died, who, had a single ounce of Peruvian bark [quinine] been properly given, might easily have escaped, in twenty-four hours, from the jaws of the grave and the disease.

Near it is a baroque draped cartouche with putti heads and a winged skull. Then comes the figure of Lady Frances Kniveton, daughter of Sir Richard Dudley, a duke of the Holy Roman Empire, even if he remained the bastard son of Queen Elizabeth's favourite, the Earl of Leicester, back in England. She lies in her shroud, which is knotted on top of her head.

Next comes a memorial in the classical Roman style, designed it is said by Inigo Jones, to the dramatist and translator **George Chapman**. He and Ben Jonson were imprisoned in 1606, in the reign of James I and VI, for their anti-Scottish remarks in the play *Eastward Ho!* on which they had collaborated, but his fame rests on his translation of Homer, and still more on the sonnet that John Keats was inspired to write, 'On First Looking into' it. He wrote this, his first great poem, in 1816, and perpetrated a famous howler by making 'stout Cortez' stare at the Pacific, 'upon a peak in Darien', when it should have been another Spanish conquistador called Balboa.

There is a cartouche on one of the pillars to **Sir Roger Lestrange** (1616–1707), who should really be commemorated in one of Fleet Street's churches since he has a good claim to be the founding father of English journalism. He was a fervent Royalist in the Civil War even to the extent of being condemned to death by the Parliamentarians in 1644. He suffered three years' imprisonment instead and as recompense was appointed 'Surveyor of the Imprimery' by Charles II at his Restoration in 1660. This post was the equivalent of being press censor (indeed Lestrange even tried to censor Andrew Marvell at one point), but it also gave him a good platform from which to publish his own periodicals such as the *Observator*, when he wasn't doing other hack work and translations. He incurred great hostility in 1680 because he was brave enough to cast doubts on Titus Oates' claims that there was a Popish Plot to stage a Catholic coup. Lestrange was accused of being a Catholic himself and forced to flee to Holland, but it was largely thanks to his efforts that Oates was eventually convicted of perjury in 1685.

On another pillar there is a tablet to Luke Hansard (d. 1828) 'Printer to the House of Commons', who has lent his name to the printed reports of parliamentary proceedings. Then, on the south side of the church interior, Mary, Countess of Kenmare who died in 1806, has a well-turned lapidary inscription by her son Viscount Castle Rosse. Under the tower and steeple there is a round vestibule, a handsome staircase leading up to the gallery, and a memorial to the sculptor John Flaxman in the form of a bronze cast of one of the many monuments he himself carved.

Once outside, turn left so that you can inspect the arch, moved from St Giles High Street in 1800. A curious tympanum has been added to it, in the form of a wooden carving of the Last Judgement. There is a number of similar ones round London, including one now on the outside wall of St Andrew, Holborn; probably they were originally placed at the entrance to church burial grounds. Christ sits in majesty above, while skeletons emerge from graves below. Hell is shown on one side, with angels playing harps and trumpets on the other. Behind the arch it will be seen that Flitcroft, with no false modesty, has 'signed' his work above the west window.

Continue southwards, past the tall, thin Elms Lesters Painting Rooms where, since 1904, backcloths for all the great theatres have been painted. Go down Flitcroft Street, past a Victorian warehouse with an eroded Gothic archway, out into the Charing Cross Road once more, past the **Phoenix Theatre** (1930) until you come to a plaque commemorating the premises of the book-sellers Marks & Co., made famous by Helene Hanff in her book *84, Charing Cross Road*. The chain bookstores cluster thickly at this point, feeding off the legendary reputation of Foyles in their midst. Their ambience is, however, far removed from the latter's porridge-tiled floors, 1960s shelving, strip lighting and extraordinary system for paying. Retrace your steps and go down Phoenix Street, to **Phoenix Garden**. This former bomb-site car park, converted in 1984, has a distinctly intimate unmunicipal feel to it, and must be invaluable in an area very short of green lungs. This shortage makes it all the odder that Camden Council's children's play area, between Phoenix Garden and St Giles churchyard, is such a dank and uninviting patch. Go through it into the churchyard because there is a tomb, by the east end of the church, of someone who played a memorable bit part in English history: **Richard Penderell**, 'Preserver and Conductor to his Sacred Majesty King Charles II . . . after his escape from Worcester Fight'. Penderell was the woodman of Boscobel in Staffordshire and he guarded the oak tree there in which Charles hid from the Roundheads who were searching for him in 1651. Later he escorted Charles when he

A Victorian warehouse in Flitcroft Street and the Phoenix Theatre stage door

A bravura shop front in New Oxford Street

escaped on a horse belonging to the Penderell family. Charles complained it was 'the heaviest dull jade he ever rode on', to which Penderell replied, 'My Liege, can you blame the horse goes heavily, when he has three Kingdoms on his back?' When visiting the National Portrait Gallery (p. 117) do not omit to see the lively sequence of pictures by Isaac Fuller, on the back staircase, showing three episodes from Charles' flight.

Penderell's tomb and epitaph, though restored in 1827, are crumbling fast, but the latter deserves to be read, for its quaint wording and central conceit of him as a star in the east.

> Hold, passenger, here's shrouded in this herse,
> Unparallel'd Pendrell. Thro' the universe,
> Like when the Eastern Star from heav'n gave light
> To three Lost Kings, so he in such dark night
> To Britain's monarch lost by adverse war
> On earth appear'd, a second eastern star ...

Condemned criminals on their way from the City to the gallows at Tyburn, at the west end of Oxford Street, used to be given a drink, the soporific 'St Giles Bowl', outside the church and later their bodies sometimes returned to be buried in the churchyard. Between 1678 and 1681 a number of Catholics falsely accused by Titus Oates were buried here after execution, including five Jesuit priests and Oliver Plunket, Archbishop of Armagh. Plunket was made a saint in 1975, but his remains had been exhumed long before.

Turn right out of the churchyard and walk to the triangular open space by the **Shaftesbury Theatre**. Built in 1911 by Bertie Crewe as the Prince's, it acquired its present name after the original Shaftesbury (now a fire station the far side of Cambridge Circus) was bombed in the last war. Its exterior is undistinguished Edwardian baroque so the visual clutter of hoardings and neon does not matter. But its auditorium is grandiose, well peopled with allegorical statuary. In 1973, just before the 2000th performance of *Hair*, a bit of the ceiling fell in and for some months there was the threat of demolition, until vociferous protest got the theatre listed in 1974. On the west side of the triangle is a wonderfully incongruous juxtaposition of an Art Deco/Egyptian office block

– inspired no doubt by the discovery of Tutankhamun's tomb in the 1920s – and the white-brick Bloomsbury Central Baptist Church in 1840s Norman style, its brutalist rose window staring balefully out on the scene.

In 1847 New Oxford Street was constructed just to the north to relieve the congestion in High Holborn and St Giles High Street, until then the only east–west route. Its other objective was to get rid of the infamous St Giles rookeries. Charles Dickens described these slums to the north of the church in *Sketches by Boz*:

Wretched houses with broken windows patched with rags and paper, every room let out to a different family and in many instances to two or even three; fruit and 'sweet-stuff' manufacturers in the cellars, barbers and red-herring vendors in the front parlours, and cobblers in the back; a bird fancier in the first floor, three families on the second, starvation in the attics, Irishmen in the passage; a 'musician' in the front kitchen, and a charwoman and five hungry children in the back one – filth everywhere – a gutter before the houses and a drain behind them – clothes drying and slops emptying from the windows.

Go north up Bloomsbury Street from the Shaftesbury Theatre and on the corner with New Oxford Street is Hazlewood House, home, as its wonderfully ornate shop front tells you, of **James Smith & Sons'** English and American Umbrella and Stick Stores (estd. 1830). You will also learn from it that they are whip makers, and suppliers of folding walking sticks, tropical sunshades, Irish blackthorns, Malacca canes, life preservers, dagger canes and swordsticks.

Go eastwards along New Oxford Street for a few yards, where a little enclosure of the houses so typical of the British Museum area to the north has penetrated to the south of the great divide. Turn southwards at the Bloomsbury Arms pub down West Central Street and then Museum Street, which soon becomes **Drury Lane**. At this north end, on the eastern side, there are two interesting businesses: at 182, Luke Hughes the furniture maker, very much in the Arts and Crafts tradition; at 181, P. O'Brien, barrow and trolley maker and hirer. Further south, at number 173, J. Sainsbury opened his first shop in the last century. Off this northern end is the site of Ashlin's Place, where the opening of some, presumably flea-ridden, merchandise imported from Holland led to the outbreak of the Great Plague in November 1664. In July of 1665 some 1361 victims were buried in St Giles churchyard alone. Cole Yard on the other side of Drury Lane (now **Stukeley Street**) was the birthplace of **Nell Gwynn**. On 1 May 1667 Samuel Pepys made one of his most evocative diary entries: 'To Westminster, in the way meeting many milkmaids with their garlands upon their pails, dancing with a fiddler before them, and saw pretty Nelly standing at her lodgings door in Drury Lane in her smock-sleeves and bodice, looking upon one – she seemed a mighty pretty creature.'

Nell had taken her first step on the way to Charles II's bed when she became an orange seller at the new theatre in Drury Lane. Charles Lamb was taken there, aged 6, in 1781 and his memories show they were still being sold at least 100 years later. 'The fashionable pronunciation of the theatrical fruiteresses then was, "Chase [choose] some oranges, chase some nonpareils [a type of apple], chase a bill of the play".' Unlike several of Charles II's other mistresses, Nell Gwynn seems to have been warm-hearted, and witty as well as quick-witted. When her coach, mistaken for that of Louise de Kérouaille – a rival mistress, was stoned by the mob, she leant out and addressed them: 'Pray, good people, be civil. I am the Protestant whore.'

Another characterful woman of the seventeenth century began life in Drury Lane. Nan Clarges was the daughter of a blacksmith and of one of five notorious women-barbers who plied their trade in the lane. She became first sempstress, then mistress, then wife of Colonel Monck. He in turn began as a Royalist officer, went over to the Parliamentarians, then was instrumental in the Restoration of Charles II, who made him Duke of Albemarle. Clarendon called her 'a woman of the lowest extraction, the least wit, and less beauty.' Nevertheless, she is credited with having kept her husband to his promise to reinstate Charles on the throne.

Abandon Drury Lane for the moment and strike eastwards along **Macklin Street**, named after a famous actor who died in 1797 and whose ghost has often appeared in front of the orchestra pit at Drury Lane Theatre (p.56). The street is 'ripe for redevelopment' as they say; turn right after a house in Gothic pink sandstone, and then left, to emerge in **Kingsway**. Turn left past number 103, which has caryatids or herms emerging from cornucopiae above its first-floor windows, to the church of **Holy Trinity** (1912). Its door is padlocked, its windows are bricked up with breeze-blocks and until recently members of the strong lager brigade were permanently encamped under its circular porch, derived surely from that on the front of St Mary-le-Strand a few hundred yards south. But a hoarding has now been erected to keep them out. What can be seen of its concave façade behind that, with empty niches topped by what look, at first glance, like one-winged angels, is a dignified piece of work by Belcher and Joass, and would have looked even better if the intended tower at its centre had got built.

Retrace your steps southward down Kingsway, looking across the street and upwards as you go, at the array of sculpture on the top of **Africa House** (1922): a lion, camel, elephant, wildebeest, crocodile and snake interspersed with two bedouin, a colonist in a pith helmet, and an African with some elephant tusks, all presided over by a centrally positioned Britannia. The pillars below have negroid faces on their capitals. Turn right into **Great Queen Street**. Sir John Summerson says in his book on *Georgian London* that this was 'the first regular street in London', but the row of houses built in about 1640, with pilasters and a continuous cornice, has long gone from the south side – the side on which James Boswell lived while writing his life of Dr Johnson. If you want to get an idea of what they looked like, nip across Kingsway to the west side of Lincoln's Inn Fields and look at numbers 59 and 60.

The south side of the street now groans under the dead weight of the headquarters of the Freemasons. 'Audi, Vide, Tace' says the inscription – hear, see, and be silent; it seems wisest to follow that injunction. The only redeeming feature is the square wedding-cake tier that crowns the corner, best seen from somewhere well to the south-west down Long Acre. There are some surviving Georgian houses on the north side of Great Queen Street and if Masonic regalia holds any sort of fascination for you, look into the windows of numbers 19 to 21 and number 22, shops which specialise in it. There will probably be a number of men in the street with funny-shaped brief cases, which house their Masonic trappings.

Cross over Drury Lane and go down Long Acre until just past

number 90, First Chicago House, one of the more repellent blocks
of the last fifteen years, and followed by an unpleasant development of red-brick shops, houses and flats on the other side of
Endell Street, into which you should now turn. This street was
created in 1844 to carry traffic northwards after it had come over
Waterloo Bridge (1817) and up Wellington Street (1834) and Bow
Street. Number 22, on the east side, was built in polychrome
Gothic brick in 1859 to house Lavers and Barraud's stained glass
works. On the west side, Latchford's timber yard front with its
red-brick pilasters against yellow brick walls, and number 71's
swags of flowers above the windows are both worth looking at.
(There also used to be an intriguing interior designer's shop called
The Study, with a sign saying it was the headquarters of the Anti
Pot-Pourri Campaign, but it has now moved to Chelsea.) Then
you come to the sober classical front of the **Eglise Suisse**. But the
best is saved until last: E. M. Barry's **St Giles National School**
(1860) at the north-western end.

The National Society for Promoting the Education of the Poor
in the Principles of the Established Church was founded in 1811.
It is instructive to compare the National School a few hundred
yards to the south, attached to St Martin-in-the-Fields and built
only thirty years earlier by Nash in his elegant classical stucco, with
the high-Victorian Gothic polychrome brick tour-de-force here.
In another decade or two, fashion had changed once more, and
the 'Queen Anne' style had become the accepted mode for the
London board schools springing up everywhere, what Sherlock
Holmes called 'Lighthouses . . . Beacons of the future.' Barry, a
son of Sir Charles Barry who built the Houses of Parliament, fresh
from his rebuilding of Covent Garden Opera House and soon to
take on the commission for the Charing Cross Hotel, built five
storeys here to accommodate 1500 children. There was a soup
kitchen in the basement, infants on the ground floor, masters' and
mistresses' residences on the mezzanine, then the girls' school,
topped by the boys'.

Go a very short way southwards down Shaftesbury Avenue
before veering to the left into **Monmouth Street** (north). You
will have noticed the increasing stylishness of the premises in
Endell Street, but fashion really starts exerting its grip from this

point on, whether in matters of eating or dressing. However, there is soon a reminder of the eternal verities in the form of an undertakers and then the Crown pub, which actually forms one of the thin ends of the wedges radiating out from Seven Dials.

The surprising, and rather confusing, street layout of **Seven Dials** is the brainchild of Sir Thomas Neale, Charles II's Master of the Mint and Groom Porter. This latter office, in which he continued until his death in about 1699, made Sir Thomas responsible, among other things, for gambling at court. He had to provide cards and dice, and to decide disputes arising at the card table and on the bowling green. This was a period full of new financial wheezes, including the National Debt and the Bank of England, and in 1694 he organised a combined lottery-and-loan for the government. A million pounds was raised, and John Evelyn's coachman won £40.

The plan no doubt looked interesting on paper, with its streets radiating out like spokes of a wheel from the central column. (There were only six streets originally, and six sundials at the top of the column.) But in reality, the scale of the layout is so small that the effect is extremely disorientating. Dickens complained about this in *Sketches by Boz*:

Look at the construction of the place. The gordian knot was all very well in its way: so was the maze of Hampton Court . . . so were the ties of stiff white neckcloths, when the difficulty of getting one on was only to be equalled by the apparent impossibility of ever getting it off again. But what involutions can compare with those of Seven Dials? Where is there such another maze of streets, courts, lanes, and alleys? Where such a pure mixture of Englishmen and Irishmen, as in this complicated part of London?

In the eighteenth century, this was the neighbourhood Hogarth depicted in his horrific print *Gin Lane*; according to Dickens, things hadn't improved that much by the 1830s.

On one side, a little crowd has collected round a couple of ladies, who having imbibed the contents of various 'three-outs' of gin and bitters in the course of the morning, have at length differed on some point of domestic arrangement, and are on the eve of settling the quarrel satisfactorily, by an appeal to blows . . . Every post in the open space has its occupant, who leans against it for hours, with listless perseverance . . .

Seven Dials

A rare survival: the ironmongers in Earlham Street

Shops for the purchase of rags, bones, old iron, and kitchen-stuff, vie in cleanliness with the bird-fanciers' and rabbit dealers' . . . Brokers' shops interspersed with announcements of day-schools, penny theatres, petition-writers, mangles, and music for balls or routs, complete the 'still life' of the subject; and dirty men, filthy women, squalid children, fluttering shuttlecocks, noisy battledores, reeking pipes, bad fruit, more than doubtful oysters, attenuated cats, depressed dogs, and anatomical fowls, are its cheerful accompaniments.

Seven Dials, like Covent Garden, escaped the plans for wholesale redevelopment in the early 1970s, but if you come in search of a picturesquely decayed enclave of the working-class virtues and vices, you are many years too late. The dedicated followers of fashion are here in force. An inscription on the column reveals that it is a new one, unveiled, rather surprisingly, by Queen Beatrix of the Netherlands in 1989. Again it only has six dials, the seventh being the column itself.

Select **Earlham Street** from the seven on offer and you will be rewarded by the two or three street barrows that survive from the good old days; also by R. Portwine the butchers at number 24, and at number 14 F. W. Collins, Ironmongers, estd. 1835. In the past the latter was 'Elastic Glue Manufacturer – sole inventor 1857' as well as 'Leather, Grindery and General Ironmonger' according to a sign on its front. It is everything such a shop should be, with as much of its stock dangling from the ceiling as is stacked on the floor or shelves. At the end of the street on the right is number 144 Shaftesbury Avenue, now a musical instrument shop but once the premises of Zaehnsdorf Ltd, craft bookbinders, as indicated by the bas-relief of a small boy so engaged, above the entrance at second-floor level.

Do not venture into Shaftesbury Avenue, but turn left into **Tower Street**. The former board school (1874) here has been done up to the highest standards to become the headquarters of Andrew Lloyd Webber's Really Useful Group. It was worth taking the trouble because the building displays many of the virtues of the 'Queen Anne' style, though its round-topped windows and primitive-classical Jacobethan doorway are not typical. At the third-floor level there are the sunflowers and lilies beloved of the Arts and Crafts movement, together with thistles and roses. Its southern end has a bas-relief panel of a guardian angel with children. Turning into **Tower Court** just beyond it, there is a row of decent Georgian houses on the right, on the left the conservatory which has been added to the school and, beyond it, the Dutch-gabled schoolmaster's house. The lean-to conservatory added to that seems less justifiable than the glass additions to the school itself.

Turn right so as to emerge into the southern part of **Monmouth Street** and immediately look to your right, where there is a fine view of the spire of St Martin-in-the-Fields framed by St Martin's Lane. The Two Brewers pub has a lively Art Deco exterior (1933), but much of the rest of the street is Georgian or early nineteenth-century. Number 67 now houses 'Deco Inspired', but most of its stock looks 1950s. Once, as the faded lettering above explains, it was the premises of B. Flegg, Saddler and Harness Maker, Horse Clothing. Number 57 has a delicate wrought-iron screen in front of its door. It is worth walking a few yards down the eastern pavement of **Upper St Martin's Lane** to look at numbers 10 to 13, four good Georgian houses belonging to the Mercers, one of the most august of the City livery companies, which has owned this area to the north of Long Acre since 1530. Then retrace your steps, averting your gaze from the looming hulk of Orion House to the west (built in 1990 but looking like something from the bad old days of the 1960s), except to notice what David Piper called in his *Companion Guide to London*, 'a rather gallant – and vast – abstract bronze by Geoffrey Clarke.' It was then (1970) 'crashed on the eastern cliff' of Thorn House, which preceded Orion House, 'as though a prehistoric cicada wrecked in a gale'. Now on the north face of the latter, it could also be likened to a badly wrapped wind-surfing board, with toasting forks and sickles added.

Curve round to the right into **Shelton Street,** by Terry Farrell's new corner building, and you will see the period premises of Comyn Ching, the architectural ironmongers, coming up on the left. Go through the arch in the middle into **Ching Court**. The sloping triangular courtyard now revealed, made up of the backs of houses in Monmouth Street, Mercer Street and Shelton Street, is a recent lively restoration also by Terry Farrell, and one of the area's pleasantest surprises. There is a new circular structure in each of the three angles and some freely interpreted 'Georgian'

Shelton Street shop fronts and Ching Court which is hidden behind them

porches on the back of the Monmouth Street houses.

Coming out from the Court, go round to the left to look at the neat Georgian former shop frontages of the **Mercer Street** houses, the roadway before them still cobbled, before going into the southern part of that street. Numbers 3, 5 and 8 are turn-of-the-century artisans' dwellings erected by the Mercers' Company in a most arresting Edwardian Baroque style. The glazed brick-work is ginger and ox blood in colour, whilst the stone doorways have broken segmental arches, and the Mercers' badge of a crowned maiden is much in evidence.

Emerge briefly into **Long Acre**, pausing only to look at number 116, Langley House, whose date (1898) and elegant treatment in terracotta and red brick make one suspect it might well be by Treadwell and Martin, who were responsible for so many good shops in the West End at this time. Notice the faces in profile, their helmets turning into ferny scrolls, or is it seaweed? At the second-floor level there are some rather androgynous full faces. Double back northwards up **Langley Street**, past Paxman the French horn specialists on the left, and the Pineapple Dance Studio on the right, until you find yourself once more in the canyon-like depths of **Shelton Street**. There is a definitive scent of Piranesi in the air at this point, with a number of sooty, satanic warehouses (the London International Film School's in particular). Go right a short way before turning left into **Neal Street**, now one of the main shopping zones around here.

A large galleria of shops under one roof, called Thomas Neal's, is housed in a former banana warehouse off to the left, which has entrances in Earlham Street and Shorts Gardens. In the same building is the **Donmar Warehouse** theatre, named after Donald Albery the impresario and his friend Margot Fonteyn. Left into **Shorts Gardens** where the shopping gets more interesting thanks to the British Cheese Shop and the Wholefood Warehouse. Notice the elaborately jokey water clock above the latter, erected by Hunkin and Plant, aquatic horologists, 1982. Minutes are indicated by the climbing water level in a vertical tube. On the hour the water is released so that it fills various containers, makes watering cans water, flowers rise up from a trough, and bells chime. Fine, as long as there's no frost. For devotees of the New Age and

Neal's Yard

British cheese in Shorts Gardens

alternative lifestyles, a canter through **Neal's Yard** behind is *de rigueur*.

You are now back at Seven Dials, where six out of the seven thin ends of the wedges forming it are trying to make some sort of architectural effort (the glass drum on top of striped brickwork is Terry Farrell again). The one that lets the side down is between Earlham Street and Mercer Street. The **Cambridge Theatre** was one of a number of new London theatres to open in 1930. Go into the foyer to see the frieze of nude dancers by Carl Toms. In 1946 the New London Opera began here before moving to Sadlers Wells; in due course it became the English National Opera at the Coliseum. Go north up Mercer Street and then across **Shaftesbury Avenue** to examine the excellent sculptural frieze by Gilbert Bayes on the MGM Cinema (once the Saville Theatre). It illustrates the history of drama and includes Romans, gladiators, a bacchanalia, the Chester Mystery Plays, St George (hidden behind the MGM fascia), 'Romance', the Twentieth Century and 'Khaki'. (Bayes was also responsible for the Queen of Time clock above the main entrance to Selfridges in Oxford Street.) Then walk westwards past number 119, home of Angels and Bermans the theatrical costumiers, and some decent terracotta and red brick buildings in the style immortalised by Osbert Lancaster as 'Pont Street Dutch'.

Just before Cambridge Circus, go left down **West Street**. On the left is the former chapel which French Protestants, the Huguenots, set up in 1700, after they fled from the persecution of Louis XIV. In 1743 John Wesley took a lease and it remained his second London centre, after that in the City Road, until he died in 1791. Next come two small theatres both built by the prolific W. G. R. Sprague (p. 33): the **Ambassadors** (1913) and **St Martin's** (1916). The former is famous as the first home of *The Mousetrap*, from 1952 until it transferred next door in 1974, where it still persists. Opposite is the Ivy Restaurant, favourite of the theatrical crowd, ringing to cries of 'Darling, you were wonderful' whenever a first-night party gathers there.

Right into **Litchfield Street** where it is worth glancing up at the plaster ceiling visible through the windows at the first-floor level of number 26. It and its two neighbours survive from the

*The MGM cinema in
Shaftesbury Avenue with
(above) part of its frieze*

The former Welsh Presbyterian Church in the Charing Cross Road

The former Cranbourn Pub in Upper St Martin's Lane, with Orion House looming behind

development of this area in the 1680s by the unscrupulous pro-moter Nicholas Barbon (p. 99). Then debouch left into the **Char-ing Cross Road**. As you do so, notice the former **Welsh Presbyterian Church**, now, ye gods, the Lamplight Disco, on the far side (1888). It is in the Norman style, often used by the Non-conformists to distinguish themselves from the Anglican Goths, and within its octagonal superstructure there is a dome. Number 74 houses **G. Smith's Noted Snuff Shop**, with its original cases full of pipes, cigars and smoker's accessories, and a permanent gas flare for customers to use as a light. Below it are one or two of the very few surviving old-style second-hand bookshops for which the street used to be famous (for number 84, see p. 14).

Great Newport Street to the left is home to the Arts Theatre and its allied Unicorn Children's Theatre, as well as the Photogra-phers' Gallery. It is where Sir Joshua Reynolds lived between 1753 and 1761, when he was building his career as England's most fash-ionable portrait painter, and you can see his house, clad in the most unsympathetic black tiles, just before the Long Island Iced Tea Shop, a cocktail bar that has colonised the Cranbourn, a Vic-torian corner pub. Go back to Leicester Square tube station, the end of this walk, via **Cranbourn Street** because above a door on the north side, just where the ox-blood tiles of the station building begin, is a plaque complete with stumps, ball and leaning bats, that used to mark the entrance to the premises of John Wisden and Co., publishers of the annual Bible for all cricket enthusiasts.

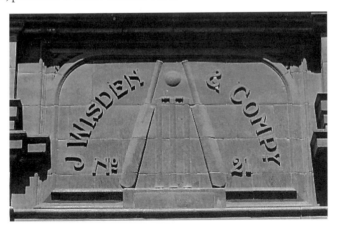

WALK TWO

Covent Garden and St Martin's Lane

Set out from Leicester Square tube southwards down the Charing Cross Road and almost immediately **Wyndham's Theatre** comes into view on the east side. Both the road and the theatre are part of a phenomenon of great importance in the later nineteenth and early twentieth-century history of London.

The story begins with the creation in 1855 of the **METRO-POLITAN BOARD OF WORKS**, not before time, to try to improve the capital's sewage and street systems. It was the period when laissez-faire liberalism was at its height, creating a very unsympathetic climate for any public body trying to get and spend public money and to cut through the special interests of the old boroughs and parishes. Undoubtedly the Board's greatest achievements were the embanking of the Thames and the sewage system associated with it (p. 89), but many of its other schemes were carried out in a penny-pinching manner, whatever the good intentions behind them. In the 1880s, shortly before the Board passed away, unlamented, to be replaced by the London County Council in 1889, it drove two new streets, Shaftesbury Avenue and the Charing Cross Road (1887), through some notorious slums. The rookeries of St Martin's were swept away by the latter, the inhabitants being rehoused in cheap new buildings erected on the narrow strips either side of the road.

One effect of these developments was to create sites on which impresarios could afford to erect new theatres catering for the increasing demand for plays or music-halls. The most famous and prolific of the new breed of specialist theatre architects who built the seductive and luxurious interiors designed to allure the audiences brought to the West End by train, cab and omnibus, was **W. G. R. SPRAGUE**. His first outstanding commission was Wyndham's Theatre in 1889, and it came from Charles Wyndham, whose

St Paul's portico with Admiral Russell's house beyond

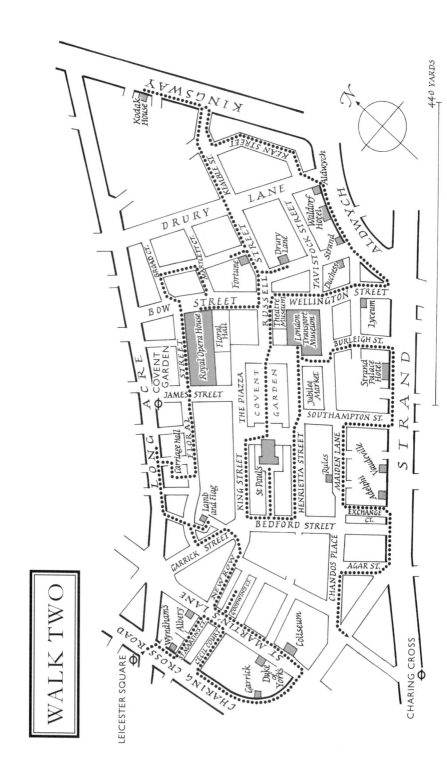

WALK TWO

company had made its name at the Criterion Theatre on Piccadilly Circus. In his later theatres, built in the 1900s, such as the Albery, Strand, Aldwych, Globe and Queen's, the influence of French beaux-arts classicism is the prevalent one, reflecting the *entente cordiale* between the two countries cemented by Edward VII. The flavour of Wyndham's is very French too, but rather than neo-classical, it is 'boudoir', Louis XV in style, with painted ceilings 'in the manner of' Boucher. The portrait medallions above the proscenium arch are of Goldsmith and Sheridan. If you cannot go into the auditorium, at least look at the decorations in the foyer.

Turn left between the white-tiled walls of **St Martin's Court**, presided over by one of London's older restaurants (estd. 1896), **Sheekey's**, which specialises in fish for theatre-goers. Josef Sheeky was an Irish fishmonger who started serving dressed crab and oysters in his Shepherd Market shop in Mayfair. The Tory prime minister of the day, Lord Salisbury, was an admiring customer and offered to let him open a rent-free restaurant on his property off St Martin's Lane. In return the Marquess could turn up at any time of the day and be served in his private rooms, but not for free. Inside, you will find Art Deco tiling by the bar and enough photographs of actors to satisfy even the most stage-struck diner.

At the St Martin's Lane end of St Martin's Court the Albery Theatre is to your left and the **Salisbury** pub to your right, traditionally much patronised by the acting profession, and as authentic a late-Victorian pub interior as you will find in London nowadays. It was also the first pub to receive the Polite Society Award in 1994 – 'the politest pub in the West End'. The **Albery**, formerly the New, was completed by Sprague in 1903, again for Charles Wyndham. Its interior is not such a gem as Wyndham's, but its theatrical history is more distinguished. Dame Sibyl Thorndike created the role of G. B. Shaw's *St Joan* here in 1924. Gielgud gave his famous *Hamlet* in 1934, and it housed the longest-ever run of *Romeo and Juliet* – 244 performances by Edith Evans and Peggy Ashcroft, with Olivier and Gielgud alternating as Romeo. When the Sadler's Wells ballet and Old Vic companies were bombed out, they moved here in 1941 and there followed some of the great Old Vic seasons.

When Leopold Mozart brought his family to London in 1764 their first lodgings were with Mr Cousin, haircutter in **Cecil Court**, into which you should turn, below the Salisbury pub. The fame of his eight-year-old prodigy son, Wolfgang, earned them a summons to Buckingham House within five days, to perform for the new king, George III, in his new palace. There, Wolfgang accompanied Queen Charlotte in an aria. A week after this the King recognised them from his carriage when they were walking in St James's Park. 'The King opened the window, leaned out and saluted us and especially our Master Wolfgang, nodding to us and waving his hand', reported Leopold. Cecil Court is almost entirely taken up with book shops and printsellers, including some specialising in such subjects as dance, or oriental religions and the occult. At all events there is good browsing, free of traffic, from which it is hard to drag oneself back into the **Charing Cross Road**.

Turn left, and as the pavement curves round, look over to the other side of Charing Cross Road. Numbers 13 and 17 are two good (very good for this street) Arts and Crafts frontages, with small leaded panes in bow windows. Number 17 is of glazed brick with an elegant wrought-iron balcony. Between them is a hideous 1950s effort, repeated behind on the east side of Leicester Square. Pevsner (*The Buildings of England: London* 1) calls it 'the more graceful variety of the modern style characteristic of progressive mid-century work.' You will soon come to the **Garrick Theatre**, financed by W. S. Gilbert from his profits as librettist of the Savoy operas and indeed designed in 1889 by **C. J. Phipps** who had been responsible for the original Savoy Theatre in 1880. Phipps was about as prolific as Sprague, with the Vaudeville in the Strand, the Lyric in Shaftesbury Avenue and Her Majesty's in the Haymarket all to his credit.

After passing the former Westminster City Hall, turn back, left, into the bottom of **ST MARTIN'S LANE**. This is a much older thoroughfare than the Charing Cross Road, and in medieval times it ran through the fields to link the two settlements of St Martin's and St Giles. In the early seventeenth century Robert Cecil, Earl of Salisbury, thanks to his powerful position as James I's chief minister, was able to circumvent the prevalent paranoia about building outside the confines of the City, and carried out what has been called the first modern property development, on his land between the Lane and Leicester Square. It seems always to have had an attraction for artists and craftsmen. The good Stuart portraitists Daniel Mytens and William Dobson lived here and the latter certainly died here in 1646. In the following century, Louis François Roubiliac, for some the greatest sculptor to have worked in Britain, had his first studio in Peter's Court (now numbers 110 and 111 on the west side). The rooms were then taken over by William Hogarth who founded the St Martin's Academy in them, the forerunner of the Royal Academy. Thomas Chippendale the furniture maker was based at number 60 on the east side while Josiah Wedgwood's house and showroom was at the junction with Newport Street.

In the later nineteenth century, the street was known as Dentists' Row. False teeth had just come in and there was window after window full of dentures. Nowadays, apart from the **Duke of York's Theatre** (1892), where *Peter Pan* was first performed in 1904, and the Albery (p. 35) higher up, St Martin's Lane is most associated with the **Coliseum**, home of the English National Opera. This was designed by **FRANK MATCHAM**, the other name among theatre architects to be spoken of in the same breath as W. G. R. Sprague. Indeed, Sprague and Bertie Crewe were both Matcham's pupils. The Hippodrome opposite Leicester Square tube was also Matcham's. For the Coliseum he chose what might be called fully inflated Edwardian Baroque. His client, the Australian-born impresario Oswald Stoll, wanted to build a bigger theatre than Drury Lane and then fill it by putting on up-market variety, four shows a day. 'Coarseness and vulgarity are not allowed at the Coliseum' ran an advertisement shortly after it opened in 1904. There was no doubting its size – its 2300 seats make it the biggest in London – nor the sophistication of its equipment. Its revolving stage, incorporating three independent turntables within it, enabled the Derby to be re-enacted with live galloping horses. But refined variety was a contradiction in terms and the place soon reverted to music-hall of the ordinary kind – Marie Lloyd's *double entendres*, Vesta Tilley's cross dressing. After 1945 it was home to a string of Broadway shows, but in 1961 it was converted to show Cinerama, the widest of the wide screens, an ignominy from which it was rescued by the arrival of opera from Sadler's Wells in 1974.

The globe at the top of its tower was planned to rotate, but safety regulations restricted it to simulated movement, an effect achieved by clever lighting inside. One ought to think of the globe as a beacon of culture glowing over the West End; instead it is more like some incandescent golf ball, teed up for a Wagnerian giant to drive towards the pin of Nelson's Column, floodlit to the south.

Some way north of the Coliseum, just beyond the Green Man and French Horn pub, there is a very easily missed passage off to the right, down which you should step for a view of **Goodwin's Court**. Quite how old its bow-fronted former shops are, is open to question. They look late eighteenth-century but, sitting there like a row of eight pouter pigeons, they are certainly well worth a glance. One up from this is **New Row**, into which you now turn. It was here, at the Pineapple, that Dr Johnson, when new to London, 'dined very well for eightpence ... It used to cost the rest a shilling, for they drank wine; but I had a cut of meat for sixpence and bread for a penny, and gave the waiter a penny; so that I was quite well served, nay, better than the rest for they gave the waiter nothing.' Past New Row's mix of smaller shops and pubs, you come to the junction of King, Garrick and Bedford Streets at its end.

This is the beginning of **COVENT GARDEN** proper. In the seventeenth century its name sometimes came out as Common Garden, but in reality it was Convent Garden, the land belonging to the Benedictine Abbot of Westminster Abbey. After Henry VIII dissolved the monasteries in the 1530s, the Duke of Somerset acquired the land. On his attainder and execution in 1550, it was then given to the 1st Earl of Bedford as a reward for his suppression of a rebellion in Devon and Cornwall. It was Francis Russell, the 4th Earl, who managed to overcome the hostility shown to any western development of London, first by Queen Elizabeth and then by the early Stuarts. He had already demonstrated his enterprise by rebuilding the family seat at Woburn in Bedfordshire (rebuilt again for the Russells by Henry Flitcroft, the architect of St Giles, in the following century), and by bringing over skilled Dutch engineers to start the drainage of the East Anglian Fens. He

The Coliseum in St Martin's Lane: the theme of casually poised human statuary has been echoed by the nearby pub

Georgian shopfronts in Goodwin's Court

was required by Charles I to pave and keep up the Long Acre road that went across the north side of his Covent Garden land, since this was the route used to go to the royal palace at Theobalds in Essex. In 1630 he petitioned to be allowed to develop Covent Garden so as to recoup his outlay.

The earl was both puritan in his religious inclinations and sympathetic to the claims of Parliament against the power of the King, but he did get consent. The only condition was that the Privy Council's own surveyor, Inigo Jones, should be used. The accepted view is that we owe the elegance and grand conception of the scheme to Jones, and in support of this there is the earl's much quoted remark to him about the new church of St Paul's, the focus of the layout: 'I wouldn't have it much better than a barn.' Inigo Jones replied, 'Well then, you should have the handsomest barn in England'. But was this not the earl expressing a natural puritan wish that a place of worship be as plain and unadorned as possible, rather than any inherent meanness or lack of vision?

When John Evelyn visited Leghorn during the Grand Tour which he took to escape the Civil War in the 1640s, he remarked in his diary, 'the Piazza is very fayre and com'odious and, with the church whose 4 columns at the portico are of black marble pol-ish'd, gave the first hint to the building both of the Church and Piazza in Covent Garden with us, tho' very imperfectly persu'd.' Most subsequent critics have not agreed with Evelyn's concluding dig, though the Italian origins of the plan, of a square surrounded by buildings with an arcade at the ground floor, have always been recognised. The label piazza may have been wrongly transferred by Londoners from the square itself to the arcades as the centuries passed (in Charleston, South Carolina, it is even applied to first-floor balconies), but what was never in doubt was the success of the venture from the start.

The arcaded terraces built on the north and east sides of the piazza became fashionable residences, despite the fact that, by the 1670s or possibly earlier, the fruit and vegetable market was get-ting established in the central area. On the south side, the aban-donment of Bedford House by the Russell family, so they could go and live on their new estate in Bloomsbury, had no ill effect. The taverns and coffee houses, the new theatre at Drury Lane opened in 1663, followed by the Covent Garden Theatre in 1732, ensured that the area became a magnet for those bent on pleasure. In May 1667 Samuel Pepys recorded:

My wife and I bethought ourselves of going to a French house to dinner, and so enquired out Monsieur Robins, my perriwigg-maker, who keeps an ordinary [offers a meal at a fixed price]; and in an ugly street in Covent Garden, did find him at the door and so we in; and in a moment almost had the table covered, and clean glasses, and all in the French manner, and a mess of potage first and then a couple of pigeons à l'esteuvé [stewed], and then a piece of boeuf-à-la-mode, all exceeding well seasoned, and to our liking; at least it would have been anywhere else but in this bad street, and in a perriwigg-maker's house, but to see the pleasant and ready attendance that we had, and all things so desirous to please, and ingenious in the people did take me mightily. Our dinner cost us 6s.

By the eighteenth century there were a number of famous brothels, like Tom and Moll King's, or Mother Douglas's. Tom King had been a scholar at Eton and verses composed on his death in 1737 claimed that

> For thee, all bawds and pimps lament,
> From every bagnio sighs are sent.

There were a number of so-called bagnios, or bath houses of ill repute, in the area. Mother Douglas features in more than one of Hogarth's satirical pictures. In 1763, that engaging rake William Hickey, still a schoolboy at Westminster, was returning to his boarding house when 'under the Piazza of Covent Garden a very pretty girl, apparently not much older than myself in years, joined me, took hold of my arm, and, looking earnestly in my face, said: "You are a fine handsome boy and too young to be walking in such a place alone, and I'll take your maidenhead." ' She was not to know that he had already made his 'first venereal attempt on a dark night in St James's Park, upon the grass', in 1762. In the same year of 1763 James Boswell, after dinner with his banker and fellow-Scot James Coutts and various friends, 'sallied forth to the Piazza in rich flow of animal spirits, and burning with fierce desire.' He met two pretty girls who agreed to drink with him in the Shakespeare's Head tavern at the south-east end of James

Street – he had no money for more than that. However, they let him 'solace my existence with them, one after the other, according to their seniority.'

Dr Johnson was no less averse than his biographer to enjoying the place. Two of his friends, Topham Beauclerk and Bennett Langton, woke him at three in the morning once,

to see if they could prevail on him to join them in a ramble . . . 'What, is it you, you dogs! I'll have a frisk with you.' He was soon drest and they sallied forth together into Covent Garden, where the greengrocers and fruiterers were beginning to arrange their hampers, just come in from the country. Johnson made some attempts to help them; but the honest gardeners stared so at his figure and manner, and odd interference, that he soon saw his services were not relished. They then repaired to one of the neighbouring taverns, and made a bowl of that liquor called *Bishop* [red wine, oranges, spices and sugar mixed], which Johnson had always liked.

J. T. Smith, sometime pupil of and model to Joseph Nollekens, the distinguished sculptor, recalled the eccentricities of his miserly master, and mistress, in *Nollekens and his Times* (1828). He remembered how, in the latter part of the eighteenth century,

One spring morning, as I was passing through Covent Garden, I was accosted by Mrs Elizabeth Carter, who had accompanied Mrs Nollekens thither for the purpose of purchasing some roots of dandelion, an infusion of which had been strongly recommended to her husband by Dr Jebb. Twigg, the Fruiterer . . . procured the roots she wanted from that class of people called 'Simplers', who sat in the centre of the garden . . . 'I recollect, Ma'am,' continued the fruiterer, 'Old Joe, who was the first person who sold flowers in this Garden: his stand was at that corner within the enclosure, then called Primrose Hill. (This spot was so named in consequence of its being the station of those persons who brought primroses to the Garden.) . . . Mrs Nollekens then requested to know which house it was in James Street, where her father's old friend, Mr Charles Grignon, resided . . . 'No. 27,' said Twigg; 'I recollect the old house when it was a shop inhabited by two old Frenchwomen, who came over here to chew paper for the *papier-mâché* people. . . . These women bought the paper-cuttings from the stationers and bookbinders, and produced it in that way, in order to keep it a secret, before they used our machine for mashing it.' *Mrs Carter.* – 'I recollect, Sir, when Mr Garrick acted, hackney-chairs were then so numerous, that they stood all round the Piazzas, down Southampton Street, and extended more than half-way along Maiden Lane, so much were they in requisition at that time.' – *Twigg.* 'Then, I suppose, Ma'am, you also recollect the shoe-blacks at every corner of the streets, whose cry was "Black your shoes, your Honour?" ' – 'Yes, Sir, perfectly well; and the clergyman of your parish walking about and visiting the fruit-shops in the garden in his canonicals; and I likewise remember a very portly woman sitting at her fruit-stall in a dress of lace, which it was said cost at least one hundred guineas, though a greater sum was often mentioned.'

In 1795 St Paul's on the west side of the Piazza was gutted by fire and then rebuilt, and by the 1820s not only had the area suffered a considerable fall from grace as the rich and fashionable moved west to Hanover, Cavendish and Grosvenor Squares, but the market arrangements were badly in need of reform. The 6th Duke of Bedford commissioned new market buildings from Charles Fowler, much as we know them today (p. 66), having been impressed by his plans for the nearby Hungerford Market (p. 79) and perhaps by those for the Duke of Northumberland's soaring iron conservatory at Syon House, also by Fowler. In 1857 Covent Garden Opera House, again as we see it now, was built after a fire in the previous theatre, by E. M. Barry (p. 52), to be followed by his Floral Hall next to it. In 1871 a new flower market began to go up in Wellington Street, where the London Transport and Theatre Museums now are. In the same decade Inigo Jones' arcaded range to the north of the Piazza was demolished, but was rebuilt, as Bedford Chambers, in what has been called a 'sympathetic paraphrase', by Henry Clutton in 1880. To the west and east, in Bedfordbury and Drury Lane, the worst of the slums were cleared and replaced by Peabody Buildings and other such 'model dwellings' for artisans. In 1904 the Jubilee Market opened on the south side of the Piazza.

The 11th Duke sold the estate shortly before the First World War and by June 1914 it belonged to Sir Joseph Beecham, owner of the Beecham's Powders business and the father of Sir Thomas the conductor, who had already masterminded a number of ground-breaking seasons at the Opera House (p. 54). The war put paid to Sir Joseph's plans to float a public company to handle the estate and his sons were left to sell off properties piecemeal. The last to go were the market buildings themselves, sold in 1962 for £4 million to the Covent Garden Market Authority, which in 1974 moved the whole operation south of the Thames to Nine Elms. Luckily this move was delayed long enough for the tide of public opinion, learning from the follies of the 1960s, to turn against the sweeping schemes of the traffic engineers and the grandiose redevelopment ideas, involving wholesale demolition, put up by the town planners. In July 1972 Barbara Cartland's daughter Raine de Chambrun – Mrs Gerald Legge, Viscountess Lewisham, Lady Dartmouth, Countess Spencer, whomever one remembers her as – became convinced that a mistake was being made and resigned as chairman of the Greater London Council committee dealing with the Covent Garden plan. Instead of street after street of Georgian and Victorian buildings vanishing, it was the plan itself that tumbled down, once she, the keystone, had gone. Sensitive restoration became the acceptable way of proceeding, and Covent Garden emerged in the 1980s, once more a magnet for pleasure seekers, as it had been two hundred years before.

Let us get back now to **Garrick Street**, an early creation of the Metropolitan Board of Works. Presiding over it, about half-way down on the left, and glorying, one feels, in its grimy exterior, is the **Garrick Club**. (The colours of the club tie, pistachio and pink, or salmon and cucumber, have perhaps been chosen as compensation for the dirt.) It began in King Street nearby in 1831 and moved here in 1864. Its membership prides itself on being drawn from less stuffy circles than those from which the clubs of Pall Mall and St James's recruit. Here are lawyers, journalists, actors, authors, publishers, but they can still blackball with the best. Bernard Levin was rejected, as was that excellent theatrical critic and diarist James Agate, who said he was not surprised since there were plenty of members who would have blackballed Garrick himself. It has a staggering collection of theatrical paintings – by Zoffany, George Clint, Sickert – but ordinary mortals wishing to see such things must wait until they get to the Theatre Museum (p. 63).

Half way up Garrick Street, turn into the beginnings of Floral Street, noticing the ingenious Gothic building on the corner, by Arthur Blomfield for Heaton, Butler and Baynes, stained glass manufacturers (1864). In fact it had begun life in 1860 as a mission house and school, before surrendering to commerce, even if of a very elevated kind. Now, of course, it is a restaurant. Almost immediately divert out of Floral Street, right past a building with a pleasingly rounded brick end, into the southern part of **Rose Street**, where lies that excellent pub the Lamb and Flag. Far too few pubs have the nerve to dispense with carpets, or to have, as this does, a medieval Latin drinking song written up on the ceiling – *Meum est propositum in taverna mori*, I mean to die in a pub. As its interior and staircase hint, it is essentially an eighteenth-century building, though refaced not long ago.

If you leave the pub via the alley called Lazenby Court there is a sign to remind you of one of the less glorious moments in English Literature – the night in December 1679 when the Poet Laureate John Dryden was beaten up by a bunch of hired thugs in Rose Street. The question is, who hired them? Was it Louise de Kérouaille, one of Charles II's mistresses, or – and this seems more likely – a fellow poet and notorious rake, John Wilmot, Earl of Rochester? Rochester had fallen out with a Lord Mulgrave in 1669 and later Dryden, who had been patronised by Rochester, transferred his allegiance to Mulgrave. In 1679 there circulated in manuscript a poem by Mulgrave called 'An Essay on Satire', which attacked Rochester and two of the King's mistresses, the Duchesses of Portsmouth and Cleveland – Louise de Kérouaille and Barbara Villiers. Contemporaries assumed it was by Dryden, but the general consensus is that it is too bad to have been his. It is infinitely sad that someone capable of writing verses like those 'On Nothing' should have stooped to employ bully boys:

> Nothing, thou elder brother even to Shade,
> Thou hadst a being ere the world was made
> And, well fixed, art of ending not afraid.

> Something, the general attribute of all,
> Severed from thee, its sole original,
> Into thy boundless self must undistinguished fall.

But by 1679 Rochester was far gone in dissipation:

*Number 30–31
Long Acre*

*Lunchtime at the
Lamb and Flag,
Rose Street*

I rise at eleven, I dine about two,
I get drunk before seven and the next thing I do
I send for my whore, when for fear of a clap
I dally about her, and spew in her lap.

J. T. Smith, in his reminiscences about Joseph Nollekens, includes a story about the sculptor's father-in-law Saunders Welch, who succeeded the famous Sir John Fielding (p. 50) in the latter part of the eighteenth century as 'one of his Majesty's Justices of the Peace for Westminster'.

When the streets were entirely paved with pebble-stones up to the houses, hackneymen could drive their coaches close to the very doors. It happened that Mr Welch had good information, that a most notorious offender, who had for some time annoyed the Londoners in their walks through the green lanes to Marylebone, and who had eluded the chase of several of his men, was in a first-floor of a house in Rose Street, Long Acre. After hiring the tallest hackney coach he could select, he mounted the box with the coachman, and when he was close against the house, he ascended the roof of the coach, threw up the sash of a first-floor window, entered the room, and actually dragged the fellow from his bed out at the window by his hair, naked as he was, upon the roof of the coach; and in that way carried the terror of the green lanes down New Street [Row], and up St Martin's Lane, amidst the huzzas of an immense throng which followed him to Litchfield Street.

By going up the northern part of Rose Street, you will emerge on **Long Acre** by Stanford's map and travel book shop, with its Dutch-gabled, leaded-lighted, Arts and Crafts frontage. It would be good to know where Richard Lovelace, that delightful Carolean poet who addressed 'Lucasta, Going to the Warres' and 'Althea, from Prison', died in Long Acre in 1657. John Aubrey merely remarked, 'He was a most beautiful gentleman. Obiit in a cellar in Long Acre, a little before the restouration of his Majestie.' Further eastwards on the south side of Long Acre, The Gap and the distinguished antiquarian booksellers Bertram Rota share number 30–31. The thin, twisted barley-sugar Venetian columns and horizontal bands of red brick make this another notable frontage. At its top can just be distinguished the words 'carriage manufacturer', the speciality of this neighbourhood in the last

*The Carriage Hall,
between Long Acre and
Floral Street*

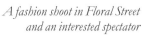

*A fashion shoot in Floral Street
and an interested spectator*

century. Indeed, if you slightly retrace your steps and go down either Banbury Court or Conduit Court you will find the **Carriage Hall** (1833) between them, recently restored by the Frederick Gibberd Architectural Partnership. In the eighteenth century this was the inn yard of the Red Lion in Floral Street, with stabling for thirty horses. But in 1806 a coach maker called Richard Turrill took over the yard on a lease from its then owners, Christ's Hospital, and it became his works. In 1832 it was destroyed by fire, and what we see is the replacement incorporating the latest in cast-iron 'fireproof' materials. This was a comparative rarity in the south, but quite common in the textile mills springing up all over the north west. Turrill was at the top of his profession and served as Master of the Coachmakers' Company in 1836. His firm remained here for the rest of the nineteenth century.

Exit from the Carriage Hall into **Floral Street** once more, and turn left. Number 19a has polychrome brick arches over its windows and cast-iron glazing bars. Number 60, now The Sanctuary women's health club, is Italianate 1860 complete with campanile and began life as the parish school. When crossing **James Street**

look at number 12, an elegant shop front, maybe by Treadwell and Martin like number 116 Long Acre (p. 26), and the Nag's Head pub next door to it on the corner, with a good terracotta horse's head on its turret. The 1980s extension to the Royal Opera House is on your right, followed by the stage door and then the entrance to the seemingly endless staircase that takes the audience up to the amphitheatre, as the gods are called.

Cross **BOW STREET** to the statue of the young dancer seated on a cane stool and tying ribbons on her shoe in **Broad Court**. It is by Enzo Plazzotta who, on this showing, was no Degas. Just by the statue is Bow Street magistrate's court and police station, here because the Fielding half-brothers, Henry the novelist and then the blind Sir John, lived in Bow Street in the middle of the eighteenth century. As Westminster magistrates, with both a police and judicial function then, they began to reform the policing of London. They relied on a good information-gathering network and were the first to employ 'thief takers' to hunt down criminals. There were six of them originally, all part-time volunteers allowed to retain any reward money and to undertake private commissions. They were the precursors of the later Bow Street Runners. Admittedly William Hickey, when writing his memoirs in the 1810s, was less than flattering about Sir John, when he recalled a brothel kept by

Mother Cocksedge, for all the Lady Abbesses were dignified with the respectable title of Mother. In these days of wonderful propriety and general morality, it will scarcely be credited that Mother Cocksedge's house was actually next, of course under the very nose of that vigilant and upright magistrate, Sir John Fielding, who, from the riotous proceedings I have been witness to at his worthy neighbour's, must have been deaf as well as blind, or at least well paid for affecting to be so.

In *Oliver Twist* Dickens brought the pickpocket, the Artful Dodger, before the magistrate at Bow Street, and later recalled, in his masterly essay 'Night Walks', from *The Uncommercial Traveller*, a sinister encounter in a coffee shop near Bow Street:

There came one morning as I sat over my houseless cup, pondering where to go next, a man in a high and long snuff-coloured coat, and shoes, and, to the best of my belief, nothing else but a hat, who took out of his hat a large cold meat pudding; a meat pudding so large that it was a very tight fit, and brought the lining of the hat out with it. This mysterious man was known by his pudding, for on his entering, the man of sleep [the coffee shop keeper] brought him a pint of hot tea, a small loaf, and a large knife and fork and plate. Left to himself in his box, he stood the pudding on the bare table, and, instead of cutting it, stabbed it, overhand, with the knife, like a mortal enemy; then took the knife out, wiped it on his sleeve, tore the pudding asunder with his fingers, and ate it all up. The remembrance of this man with the pudding remains with me as the remembrance of the most spectral person my houselessness encountered. Twice only was I in that establishment, and twice I saw him stalk in (as I should say, just out of bed, and presently going back to bed), take out his pudding, stab his pudding, wipe the dagger, and eat his pudding all up. He was a man whose figure promised cadaverousness, but who had an excessively red face, though shaped like a horse's. On the second occasion of my seeing him, he said huskily to the man of sleep, "Am I red tonight?" "You are," he uncompromisingly answered. "My Mother," said the spectre, "was a red-faced woman that liked drink, and I looked at her hard when she laid in her coffin, and I took the complexion." Somehow, the pudding seemed an unwholesome pudding after that, and I put myself in its way no more.

About one hundred years before, when the gin craze was at its height in London, a Bow Street tavern proclaimed 'Here you may get drunk for a penny, dead drunk for twopence, and get straw for nothing.'

Broad Court has some good Queen Anne style buildings to look at on its north side before turning right into Crown Court and right again into **Martlett Court**. In the mid-eighteenth century this was the home of the comedian Ned Shuter, who once said he would rather have twenty holes than one darn in his stocking, because 'a hole is an accident of a day, but a darn is premeditated poverty'. Later the actress Harriot Mellon lived here. The banker Thomas Coutts (p. 106) married her when he was eighty and, since his three daughters were well provided for, left her all his money. She then married the Duke of St Albans and when she in turn died, left her fortune of £80,000 a year to one of Coutts' granddaughters, Angela Burdett. As Baroness Burdett Coutts, she was one of the great philanthropists of the Victorian age.

You should now be standing on the pavement opposite the **ROYAL OPERA HOUSE**. The first theatre here was opened in 1732 by John Rich, previously proprietor of the Theatre Royal in Lincoln's Inn Fields (p. 56). There John Gay's *Beggars' Opera* had 'made Gay rich and Rich gay'. The profits from this and from a revival of *Dr Faustus*, together with some public subscriptions, paid for the Covent Garden Theatre Royal. Rich was associated with Handel, and opera alternated with plays. Both *She Stoops To Conquer* and *The Rivals* had their first nights here. In 1789 the cantankerous old actor Macklin appeared for the last time. He had been born in 1700 and many years before had earned notoriety for killing another actor in a quarrel over a wig. John Philip Kemble, brother of the actress Mrs Siddons, brought a sixth share of the business in 1803, and in 1808 the theatre burnt down. When Kemble tried to raise prices at the opening of the new theatre, designed by Robert Smirke, in 1809, there were O.P. (old price) riots for the following sixty-one nights, until he climbed down. William Hazlitt described the lobbies of the theatre, not long after this, full of half-naked prostitutes soliciting. He claimed they were in the clutches of elderly Jewish women clothes dealers from whom they hired their dresses for the evening.

The theatre interior was reconstructed along the lines of La Scala in Milan in 1847 and reopened as the Italian Opera House. Until 1843 Her Majesty's Theatre in the Haymarket had had the monopoly of performing Italian opera, but now lost much of its audience and many of its singers to Covent Garden. In 1856 it burnt down again, after a rather dissolute masked ball was held. E. M. Barry rebuilt it very much in the spirit of Smirke's theatre, reusing Flaxman's bas-reliefs and Rossi's statues of the Muses of Comedy and Tragedy on the front. It re-opened in 1858 as the Royal Italian Opera, but in 1888 Augustus Harris, the Drury Lane impresario, had to come to its rescue, which he effected in part by introducing operas in languages other than Italian. Barry's porte cochère was enclosed and something rather like a large white railway carriage was added under the portico at first-floor level to house the bar-space of the Crush Bar.

Mahler conducted Wagner's Ring here in 1892; Nellie Melba sang in nearly every season up to 1914. In Thomas Beecham's first

The Royal Opera House

Drury Lane Theatre, the colonnade

season he staged the first British performance of Richard Strauss's *Elektra*. 'Excepting the death of King Edward, which occurred in the following spring, it was the most discussed event of the year,' he claimed. He followed up with Strauss's *Salome*; and then *Rosenkavalier* and Stravinsky's ballet *Petrushka* in the same season. Bruno Walter was the chief conductor in the 1920s and Beecham once more in the 1930s. During the Second World War the Opera House became a dance hall but revived afterwards, thanks to increasing levels of state subsidy. Since 1946 the Opera House has also been home to ballet. Ninette de Valois' Sadler's Wells company transferred then, changing its name to the Royal Ballet in 1956.

It would be ridiculous to claim intimacy as a quality of the Opera House, but it is less overbearing than the Paris Opera or La Scala. Its staircase is generous and the Crush Bar chandelier is a whopper, but once inside the auditorium the pervading atmosphere is of warmth and inclusion. Perhaps it is the five-branched claret-shaded sconces lighting the horseshoe, and interspersed with bare-breasted maidens. The curtains have the monogram E II R embroidered on them in the heaviest bullion, there is the royal coat of arms above them and then, in case the message of royal patronage has still escaped you, there is a medallion of the young Queen Victoria surrounded by a scene of Orpheus playing his lyre in bas-relief. Over all, there is the blue saucer-dome. In *The Waves*, Virginia Woolf likened the audience sorting themselves out in the stalls to 'birds settling in a field' and described how 'the whole house glowed – red, gold, cream-coloured'. How much of that glow is due to pleasurable anticipation and how much to the decoration, is of little account.

Immediately to the left of the Opera House is the **Floral Hall** built by E. M. Barry at the same time. They make strange neighbours, with Corinthian columns next to Crystal Palace-inspired cast-iron and glass. It opened for trading in 1861, but soon changed from flowers to fruit auctions, necessitating the building of a Flower Market further south down Wellington Street. The Floral Hall had a dome and curved roof but these had to be dismantled after a fire in 1956. It is incorporated in the latest scheme for developing the Opera House, but alas without a new dome

and with the loss of the portico fronting the Piazza. The development should begin in 1997 and will cost £214 million (£23 million
has already been spent). The Floral Hall will become 'the principal
foyer space' while the amphitheatre (the gods), where there will be
another foyer, will no longer be segregated from the rest of the
building, but linked with the Floral Hall by escalators. There will
be no great increase in the number of seats but the back-stage will
be transformed, not before time. The electric motors running the
stage lifts date from before 1914. The areas between the Floral
Hall and James Street and to the south of the Hall down to Russell
Street will be built up, including a new 500-seat theatre. The north-
east corner of the Piazza will once more have an arcade round it
and a new passage-arcade will be created linking this corner with
Bow Street. The only commercial element will be the ground-
floor shops, while there will be a loggia looking down on to the
Piazza. The most likely temporary home for the opera and ballet,
while this development goes on, was to have been a new auditorium planned for an empty site in Southwark by Tower Bridge, but
this is now in doubt.

On the other side of Bow Street to the Floral Hall is the deeply
ugly 1960s extension to the 1920s telephone exchange in **Russell
Street**, into which now turn left. The second-floor windows of
the exchange here are a curiosity, the columns and pediments of
their aedicules having no visible means of support, but it is a hundred times preferable to the extension. Russell Street was famous
as the location of Will's Coffee House, where Dryden held court
and which John Dennis mocked:

> To Will's I went where Beau and Wit
> In mutual contemplation sit;
> But which were Wits, and which were Beaus,
> The Devil's sure in him who knows,
> For either may be which you please,
> These look like those who talk'd like these.

Later there was Button's Coffee House. Joseph Addison of the
Spectator set up Daniel Button in business in 1712 and it rapidly
became the new centre of the literary world. Next to the
exchange is the **Fortune Theatre** built in 1924 and bizarrely

incorporating an entrance to the Crown Court Church of Scotland, which lies behind it. Notice the minuscule box office all covered in shiny brass and the nude statue of yet another Muse above the entrance.

On the other side of the road is the **THEATRE ROYAL, DRURY LANE**. It owes its origin to Charles II adopting at his Restoration one of his father's bad habits, which had led to the outbreak of the Civil War in 1642: the granting of monopolies. In this case he gave two of his courtiers, Sir William Davenant and **Thomas Killigrew**, the exclusive right to stage plays in London; Davenant opened a theatre in Lincoln's Inn Fields, while Killigrew did the same at Drury Lane in 1663. (In time Davenant's 'patent' was transferred to Covent Garden, see page 52. The monopoly only ended in 1843.) Pepys called Killigrew 'a merry droll, but a gentleman of great esteem with the King'. By 1667 he was reporting, 'Tom Killigrew hath a fee out of the Wardrobe for cap and bells under the title of King's jester, and may revile or geere anybody, the greatest person without offence, by the privilege of his place.' But in 1669 this proved not to be the case as far as the Earl of Rochester was concerned: 'Among the rest of the king's company, there was that worthy fellow Tom Killigrew whose mirth and raillery offended the former [Rochester] so much, that he did give Tom Killigrew a box on the ear in the King's presence, which do give much offence to the people here at court, to see how cheap the King makes himself.' Rochester was drunk, as usual.

Nell Gwynn's early days at Drury Lane have already been touched on (p. 18). Her first lover was the actor Charles Hart, grand-nephew of Shakespeare, but in 1665 she caught the eye of the King when performing here in Dryden's tragedy *The Indian Emperor*. An anonymous contemporary described her as 'red-haired and rather *embonpoint* . . . she had remarkably lively eyes, but so small they were almost invisible when she laughed; and a foot the least of any woman in England.' Pepys reported that 'to see how Nelly cursed for having so few people in the pit was very pretty'.

When his first theatre burnt down, Killigrew got Christopher Wren to design a much bigger 2500-seater, which lasted until 1791, though modified by Robert Adam for **David Garrick**. He did not suffer any difficulty in filling the pit, as James Boswell reported in 1763.

> I went to Drury Lane and saw Mr Garrick's play King Lear. So very high is his reputation, even after playing so long, that the pit was full ten minutes after four although the play did not begin till half an hour after six. I kept myself at a distance from all my acquaintances and got into a proper frame . . . I was fully moved and shed an abundance of tears.

Later that year Boswell admitted to 'the wild peak of youthful extravagance' when, sitting in the pit at Drury Lane, he 'entertained the audience prodigiously by imitating the lowing of a cow'. **Richard Brinsley Sheridan** succeeded Garrick as manager in 1776, and in 1777 his play *The School for Scandal* had its first performance at Drury Lane. The new theatre designed, by Henry Holland, opened in 1794, only to burn down in 1809. His friends found Sheridan watching the flames from a neighbouring tavern with a drink in his hand. When they expressed surprise, he retorted, 'Cannot a man enjoy a glass of wine by his own fireside?' Sheridan was in no position to rebuild the theatre and the task was taken on by the radical MP and brewer, Samuel Whitbread, who employed Benjamin Wyatt as architect. Lord Byron was on the management committee and wrote an indifferent poetical address for the re-opening in 1812. The first performance of Edmund Kean in 1814 – as Shylock in *The Merchant of Venice* – gave a great fillip, and he continued to electrify audiences into the 1820s.

The rather foursquare portico was added to the front of the building in 1820 and the Russell Street colonnade in 1831. Its Ionic columns are made of cast-iron and although painted blue now, they began life bright maroon, which led to the nickname of Rhubarb Alley. The wrought-iron gas lamp supports have a bravura swoop to them. Two of the side doors have the royal coat of arms above them; and look out also for the good brickwork of the niche above the stage door. Among the scenery painters at this time were two who went on to make considerable names as artists: David Roberts, renowned for his views of Egypt and the Holy Land, and Clarkson Stanfield, the marine painter.

From 1841 to 1851 the tragedian William Macready managed Drury Lane, but it reached the height of its prosperity under **Sir**

Augustus Harris (1879–97) and then Arthur Collins. The former, nicknamed Druriolanus, has a gruesome shrine, incorporating a drinking fountain, on the left of the theatre's front. Spectacular effects – undersea divers, *Carmen* with real bulls, *Ben-Hur* with a real chariot race, elephants on stage – and the lavish Drury Lane pantomimes are what they are remembered for. Cameron Mackintosh's helicopter in *Miss Saigon* is nothing new. The big stars from the music halls were recruited for the pantos and Osbert Sitwell recalled watching the comedian 'Dan Leno as the beautiful duchess, wearing a hooped dress and a large picture hat with a feather flowing from the brim, fall through the harp he was playing. I can still remember vividly that supreme representation of artistic abandon.'

In 1913 Thomas Beecham's father collaborated with Sergei Diaghilev to bring Russian opera and ballet here. The 1930s were Ivor Novello's years, and then after 1945 a string of huge American musical successes began with *Oklahoma*.

The entrance vestibule, the rotunda beyond it, the staircase off to each side of the rotunda and the domed foyer above it are well worth seeing, though the auditorium has been rebuilt. If you want to inspect the venerable stage machinery, or hear about the ghosts and the Baddeley Cake, there are regular guided backstage tours each day. The actor Robert Baddeley died in 1784, leaving money to be spent on a cake for 'the ladies and gentlemen performers' each Twelfth Night, while the most famous ghost is the Man in Grey, an eighteenth-century figure who appears only during matinées in the Upper Circle. If he materialises before a first night, it is a very good omen. Actors giving a bad performance are said to feel a kick in the bottom from the early nineteenth-century clown, Joseph Grimaldi.

Before leaving **Catherine Street**, where Drury Lane Theatre really is, look at number 33, the green and rather lopsided Suttons Seeds shop. The Duchess Theatre to the south is one of the least distinguished architecturally. John Gay once hymned the harlots

> . . . who nightly stand
> where Katherine Street descends to the Strand . . .
> With flatt'ring sounds she soothes the cred'lous ear
> My noble captain! Charmer! Love! My dear!

*Drury Lane Theatre,
the portico*

*Restaurants in
Catherine street*

At the east end of Russell Street, by the ugly multi-coloured post-
modern building, turn left into Drury Lane for a few yards, for a
glimpse of a very small public garden, formerly an old burial
ground belonging to St Martin-in-the-Fields. The little buildings
either side were the mortuary and keeper's cottage. There is argument on the point, but this could be the burial ground that Lady
Dedlock, in Dickens' *Bleak House*, paid Jo the crossing sweeper to
show her, since it contained the body of her former lover, 'Nemo'.

'There!' says Jo, pointing. 'Over yinder. Among them piles of bones, and
close to that there kitchin winder! they put him wery nigh the top. They
was obliged to stamp up on it to git it in. I could unkiver it with my
broom, if the gate was open. That's why they locks it, I s'pose,' giving it a
shake. 'It's always locked. Look at the rat!' cries Jo, excited. 'Hi! Look!
There he goes! Ho! Into the ground!'

The continuation of Russell Street eastwards is called **Kemble
Street**, with some grim, grey Peabody Buildings on the left, but a
good 1907 hostel for single working men, called **Bruce House,**
on the right. It has elegant Art Nouveau railings and a continental
feel to its roof line, and has recently been repaired to house and
train 200 homeless young people. The round **Space House** further on is instantly recognisable as Seifert's, working again for
Harry Hyams, and shares its inspiration with the former's Shera-
ton Park Tower Hotel at Knightsbridge.

Kemble Street ends in **Kingsway** and, if you turn left into it and
walk to the next block, you will find number 65, **Kodak House**,
built in 1911 in a pared down, simplified style, and regarded as a sig-
nificant harbinger of so much that was to follow in the way of commercial architecture. Its architect, Sir John Burnet, was also
building the Edward VII Galleries on the northern side of the
British Museum at this time, with their pure Ionic colonnade.
Retrace your steps into Kemble Street, and make up for the visual
aridity of Space House and Kodak House by looking at the
merman and mermaid above the entrance to the Leeds Building
Society on the corner, and the jolly garden temple perched on top
of the block. Turn left into **Kean Street** where Aram Designs
occupy a handsome Arts and Crafts corner warehouse and their
showroom acts as the equivalent of a modern furniture museum.

From the southern end of Kean Street the **Aldwych Theatre** can be seen on the corner of Drury Lane. It, together with its near-twin, the Strand Theatre, and the Waldorf Hotel in between, make an impressive unified frontage. It is best seen from the western end of the Aldwych 'island', site of the late lamented Gaiety Theatre which, together with Inveresk House (see below), made this perhaps the best group of Edwardian buildings in London, erected as part of the scheme which created Kingsway. Both the Aldwych and the **Strand Theatre** were built by W. G. R. Sprague in 1905. While the interior of the Aldwych, with its circular gallery from which one can look down into the entrance hall, is more interesting, the exterior of the Strand has much more sculptural detail. From the 1960s until 1982 the Aldwych was the London base of the Royal Shakespeare Company, so saw such productions as Peter Brook's *Midsummer Night's Dream* and *Nicholas Nickleby*. The Strand's roll-call is less distinguished, burdened by eleven years of *No Sex Please, We're British*.

The Waldorf Hotel has giant Corinthian columns with large putti above them busy sculpting, painting, making music, to impress its guests. It has also kept its palm court, a good spot for a reviving cup of tea, even for a *thé dansant* or a tango on certain afternoons. Beyond the Strand Theatre is **Inveresk House**, built in 1907 by Mewès and Davis for *The Morning Post* newspaper in the refined Parisian classical style that they had already displayed at the Ritz in Piccadilly. The extra floor added to it has done it no favours—let us hope it gets a sympathetic new tenant to enliven its current moribund state.

Turn north up **Wellington Street** and there on the left is the portico of the **Lyceum Theatre** designed in 1834 by Samuel Beazley who was also responsible for the Drury Lane Theatre colonnade. The rest of the theatre was rebuilt in 1904 and now, after many years of neglect, is being restored. The Lyceum is indissolubly linked with the régime of **Sir Henry Irving**, who dominated the Victorian stage from the 1870s until 1901, and was financed initially by Baroness Burdett Coutts. Shortly after his death Max Beerbohm summed up Irving's strengths and weaknesses:

It was as a producer of Shakespeare that Irving was great in management. He was the first man to give Shakespeare a setting contrived with

*An elegant warehouse
in Kean Street*

*The Waldorf Hotel
Palm Court*

archaic and aesthetic care . . . Of course spectacle may be overdone. Irving may sometimes have overdone it; but he always overdid it beautifully . . . As philosopher or king, poet or prelate, he was matchless. One felt that if Charles the Martyr, Dante, Wolsey, were not precisely as he was, so much the worse for Wolsey, Dante, Charles the Martyr.

Irving (born Henry Brodribb) was assisted by the matchless Ellen Terry, 'Our Lady of the Lyceum' as Oscar Wilde called her. She was the least stagey or artificial of actresses, giving the impression to W. Graham Robertson when he first met her of having 'stepped in from some dim garden, her arms full of lavender and lad's love and bringing with her a freshness, a breeze from the open sky.' This made her a perfect foil to Irving. The third member of the triumvirate was the theatre's manager, Bram Stoker, remembered now as the author of *Dracula*.

At number 26 Wellington Street Dickens published his magazine *All The Year Round* and Wilkie Collins was on the staff when his novel *The Moonstone* was serialised in it. He dictated this in 1868 while heavily under the influence of opium and, indeed, its plot hinges on the effects of the drug. Divert for a moment, right into Henrietta Street, and there you will find number 36 where Thomas de Quincey lived when he was writing his *Confessions of an English Opium Eater* published in 1821. Then on northwards past the giant fanlight windows of the old **Flower Market** before turning left into **Russell Street** once more, by the Market's lively octagonal corner turret with its urns, balustrade and cupola. There is a blue plaque on what was Thomas Davies' bookshop where Boswell met Johnson for the first time in 1763 and survived a series of devastating put-downs. 'I come from Scotland, but I cannot help it', said Boswell, to be met by Johnson's retort, 'Sir, that, I find, is what a great many of your countrymen cannot help.'

This is just by the entrance to the **Theatre Museum** which shares the Market building with the London Transport Museum. The ground-floor display area will, in all probability, have completely altered by the time this book appears, but down the ramp will be found such items as Thomas Killigrew's original patent (p. 56), Mrs Siddons' dressing table, Tom Thumb's waistcoat, costumes from the original 1913 Paris production of Stravinsky's

Rite of Spring (the Museum has a mass of Diaghilev ballet costumes stored away), and Noël Coward's dressing gown. There is an out-standing collection of theatrical paintings assembled by Somerset Maugham, a small theatre, the National Video Archive of Stage Performances recorded simultaneously with up to four cameras, and an exhibition called 'Slap', about theatrical make-up, with experts on hand to show you how to apply it to yourself on the spot (or over them, as the case may be). The current centrepiece is an elaborate display about all aspects of the Royal National The-atre production of Alan Bennett's dramatisation of *The Wind In The Willows*, even down to coaching the cast in suitable animal movement, using films of stoats, weasels, etc.

The **PIAZZA** opens up at the west end of Russell Street and the buildings of **COVENT GARDEN MARKET** proper occupy its centre. In its eighteenth- and nineteenth-century heyday, the Mar-ket was a natural topic for writers. Here are two views, the first unattractive, the second more inviting. Tobias Smollett, always stimulated by the more rancid side of life, described it in *Humphrey Clinker* (1771):

I saw a dirty barrow-bunter in the street, cleaning her dusty fruit with her own spittle, and who knows but some fine lady of St James's parish might admit into her delicate mouth those very cherries, which had been rolled and moistened between the filthy, and perhaps ulcerated, chops of a St Giles huckster – I need not dwell on the pallid contaminated mash which they call strawberries.

Henry Mayhew gave a vivid panorama of the Market in the 1850s in his *London Labour and the London Poor*:

Under the dark Piazza little bright dots of gas-lights are seen burning in the shops; and in the paved square the people pass and cross each other in all directions, hampers clash together, and excepting the carters from the country, every one is on the move. Sometimes a huge column of bas-kets is seen in the air, and walks away in a marvellously steady manner, or a monster railway van, laden with sieves of fruit, and with the driver perched up on his high seat, jolts heavily over the stones . . . Wagons, with their shafts sticking up in the air, are ranged before the salesmen's shops, the high green load railed in with hurdles, and every here and there bunches of turnips are seen flying in the air over the heads of the

*Cupola on the corner of
the old Flower Market,
Covent Garden*

*Floral Hall: the Piazza
frontage threatened with
demolition*

people. Groups of apple-women, with straw pads on their crushed bonnets, and coarse shawls crossing their bosoms, sit on their porter's knots, chatting in Irish, and smoking short pipes; every passer-by is hailed with the cry of, "want a baskit, yer honor?" The porter, trembling under the piled-up hamper, trots along the street, with his teeth clenched and shirt wet with the weight, and staggering at every step he takes.

The broccoli tied up in square packets, the white heads tinged slightly red, as it were, with the sunshine, – the sieves of crimson love-apples, polished like china, – the bundles of white glossy leeks, their roots dangling like fringe, – the celery, with its pinky stalks and bright green tops, – the dark purple pickling-cabbages, – the scarlet carrots, – the white knobs of turnips, – the bright yellow balls of oranges, and the rich brown coats of chestnuts – attract the eye on every side. . . . The walnut merchant, with the group of women before his shop, peeling the fruit, their fingers stained deep brown, is busy with the Irish purchasers. The onion stores, too, are surrounded by Hibernians, feeling and pressing the gold-coloured roots, whose dry skins crackle as they are handled. Cases of lemons in their white paper jackets, and blue grapes, just seen above the sawdust are ranged about, and in some places the ground is slippery as ice from the refuse leaves and walnut husks scattered over the pavement.

Against the railings of St Paul's Church are hung baskets and slippers for sale, and near the public-house is a party of countrymen preparing their bunches of pretty coloured grass – brown and glittering, as if it had been bronzed. Between the spikes of the railing are piled up square cakes of green turf for larks; and at the pump, boys, who probably have passed the previous night in the baskets about the market, are washing, and the water dripping from their hair that hangs in points over the face.

Under the Piazza the costers purchase their flowers (in pots) which they exchange in the streets for old clothes. . . . Men and women, selling different articles, walk about under the cover of the colonnade. One has seed-cake, another small-tooth and other combs, others old caps, or pig's feet, and one hawker of knives, razors, and short hatchets, may occasionally be seen driving a bargain with a countryman, who stands passing his thumb over the blade to test its keenness. . . . The pump in the market is now surrounded by a cluster of chattering wenches quarrelling over whose turn it is to water their drooping violets, and on the steps of Covent Garden Theatre are seated the shoeless girls, tying up the halfpenny and penny bundles.

Charles Fowler's central buildings were completed by 1830 and cost £70,000, twice the estimate, but in the long term proved a sound investment for the Bedford Estate. Looking at the quality of the granite flooring, pitted and scored to give the horses a grip, and of the Greek Doric granite columns, one can see where the money went. The Central Avenue was always roofed, and lined on both sides with retail shops selling fruit and flowers. The conservatories on the roof were prototype garden centres. Originally the North and South Halls, where the growers came to sell their produce wholesale, were not roofed. The shopkeepers wanted things to stay like this, making conditions as uncomfortable as possible so that the growers would not be tempted to stay and muscle in on the retail trade. But the growers got roofs in the 1870s and 80s. In the 1970s, when the time came to restore and convert the buildings, an argument developed between the Georgian Group and the Victorian Society as to whether these roofs should stay or go. The Victorian Society, with the British weather on its side, won and the roofs stayed.

The problems of what to do with various basements and how to increase lettable space so as to bring in sufficient rent were solved by digging out the two courtyards in the South Hall, before the whole complex was opened once more in 1980. The Central Avenue seems to be something of a monoculture of shoe shops now, but things get more interesting in the North Hall where the east end is given over to street entertainers – a man in a crash helmet spinning on his head, for example. The west end is called the Apple Market and reserved for small stalls selling crafts, jewellery, hand-knits. In the eastern of the two courtyards dug out in the South Hall, there are normally some musicians playing or singers singing. Here you will also find the Cabaret Mechanical Theatre which is full of animated, kinetic toys and displays, good for children. Apart from all this, and the regular shops and cafés, there are antique stalls every Monday and the first Sunday of the month, and an art market on the second and last Sundays of the month. The open space to the west, in front of St Paul's portico, is the other big pitch for the street entertainers – the usual mix of fire-eating mono-cyclists, mime artists and jugglers.

It is easy to sneer at the Piazza as a homogenised, Disneyfied affair and regret the departure of the cockneys and cabbage stalks. But if your mood is right, the sun is shining and the scene

Fowler's Central Market building, Covent Garden

The old Westminster Fire Office, now Moss Bros, King Street, Covent Garden

animated, it is just as easy to enjoy it. One thing is certain, it beats Oxford Street any day.

To the north of Fowler's buildings there is a group of open-air stalls on a site which will be absorbed into the Opera House development, but which in the eighteenth century was the location of the Shakespeare's Head Tavern. Its owner, one Tomkyns, was famous for his turtle soup. He ordered fifty of them at a time and then despatched the soup all over the country to the houses of the gentry. To the west of it are Clutton's Bedford Chambers (p. 43), which have a glass-roofed courtyard behind, lined with glazed white brick. The measure of visual unity at this end of the Piazza owes much to Clutton, who also built numbers 1 to 4 King Street (Doc Martens shop), numbers 41 and 42 opposite, and the twin to numbers 1 to 4, number 34 Henrietta Street (NatWest) to the south of St Paul's. The tone which he set continues in other buildings to the south and east of the Piazza.

The Tuscan columns and pillars of **St Paul's Portico** are about all that remains of Inigo Jones' original fabric, after the fire of 1795 and the re-facing of the body of the church in hard brick in the 1870s. But the contrast between the wooden eaves overhead and the stone, the two heroic gas lamps under the portico, and the consciousness that it was here Punch and Judy first performed in England, that here Professor Higgins first encountered Eliza Doolittle and became ensnared by the awful fascination of her vowel sounds, all make it worth a pause. One of the matching gateways either side of the portico has been restored and the other is now being built. It will incorporate the entrance to the underground lavatories and also sport a fountain.

The most interesting building in **King Street** is number 43, with its pink front punctuated by large pilasters. It was built about 1716, probably by Thomas Archer, the architect of St John's, Smith Square, in Westminster for his client **Admiral Edward Russell**, latterly Earl of Orford. It has been much altered over the years but it keeps the baroque flag flying next to Jones' more strictly classical temple. Russell was a younger brother of the 1st Duke of Bedford. He fought at the Battle of Solebay in 1672, but was no friend of Samuel Pepys, Secretary to the Admiralty, who regarded him as one of those 'gentlemen captains' who stood in the way of his attempts to professionalise the Royal Navy. Russell, for his part, was in deep with those out to ruin Pepys in 1679, at the time of the Popish Plot, because the diarist was a protégé of the catholic James, Duke of York. The pendulum swung the other way in 1683 and Russell's cousin, Lord William Russell, was executed for implication in the Rye House Plot against James and Charles II; the Admiral then became one of the chief engineers behind the Glorious Revolution of 1688, when James was ousted by William of Orange. But Russell was ambitious and arrogant, quite capable of intriguing with James, exiled in France, and at the same time leading the fleet which defeated the French at La Hogue in 1692.

In 1790 the house became Evans Hotel and Supper Rooms, famous for its poached eggs on steak and devilled kidneys seasoned with red pepper; famous, too, as an early precursor of the music-halls, because of the entertainment it offered. Choristers from the Savoy Chapel sang glees and part songs, and were followed by comic vocalists. Later it housed the National Sporting Club where nobs in evening dress watched boxing.

Thomas Arne, composer of 'Rule Britannia', was born at number 31 King Street. Coleridge lodged at number 10 in November 1801, escaping from the Lakeland winter and from his wife, whilst he wrote journalism for the *Morning Post*: 'I saw so many people and walked to and fro so much that I have been . . . like a fish in air . . . panting and dying from excess of oxygen.' The large portcullis on Moss Bros' shop, repeated in its railings, indicates that the building used to be the Westminster Fire Office (insurance), not that the Houses of Parliament have diversified into gents' dress hire. Turn left by it down **Bedford Street**, once thick with publishers: Macmillan issued *Alice in Wonderland* from number 16 in 1865, Frederick Warne published Beatrix Potter's books from number 15, and J. M. Dent the Everyman Library from number 29. Frank Swinnerton mischievously recalled how 'J. M. Dent was a very emotional man. One day I went into his office when he was signing authors' royalty cheques and the tears were running down his cheeks.' The entrance to **St Paul's** churchyard is a little way down on the left. The grass, flower beds, benches and gas lamps are overlooked by tall buildings on three sides, with the west front of the church on the fourth. The interior of St Paul's gives an impression of uncluttered width – no aisles, no columns, no galleries except at the west end. It is lined with fairly standardised black wooden memorial plaques to actors, dancers and entertainers. The casket containing the ashes of Ellen Terry on the south wall is worth hunting down.

Before turning left into Henrietta Street, look further down Bedford Street to the good Edwardian Baroque building on the corner with Chandos Place, its turret topped by a copper urn, and the offices of *The Lady* magazine opposite. **Henrietta Street** had its publishers too: the left-wing autocrat Victor Gollancz at number 14, and Gerald Duckworth at number 3. Duckworth was half-brother to Virginia Woolf and may, or may not, have interfered with her when she was a child, but the novelist Anthony Powell, who worked for him, says 'His interest in books, anyway as a medium for reading, was as slender as that of any man I have ever encountered.' Powell goes on to describe the office, with a

door inscribed with the name of the firm; possibly followed by the word ENQUIRIES, though I am not sure about that. If so, the hope was not one to build on. Within . . . three or four breezy young men, invoice clerks, would be engaged in caustic conversation among themselves at their long high desk . . . and their attention had to be caught.

In 1813 Jane Austen stayed for a few weeks at number 10 with her brother, who worked in a bank. Look at the faint lettering on Fowler's corner building here: Jas Butler Herbalist, Seedsman, Lavender Water.

At the end of Henrietta Street there is the new Jubilee Market Hall, embellished, if that is the word, with some jagged slabs of multi-coloured rock with a bell in a hole cut into the stone. The actual **Jubilee Market** is beyond: the place to go, with its cheap-and-cheerful stalls, if you are suffering from fatigue of the good-taste buds.

The entrance to the **LONDON TRANSPORT MUSEUM** comes next. Given all those shiny red buses, trams and trains, this was always going to be a winner, and since its £4 million revamp it is even better, with a clever new mezzanine floor to allow more vehicles to be displayed. It is now equipped with 'touch-screen interactives', 'visitor-driven simulators' and 'video walls', but for

me the best add-on exhibit was a lovely documentary made in
1952 about the last of the London trams, called 'Riding on Top of
the Car' after the wonderful music-hall song, which forms part of
the sound track.

You will learn that each horse bus required at least twelve
horses, working in pairs, to keep it on the road for fourteen hours
a day. Think of the quantities of dung that entailed. One is told
also, with nice irony, that the average traffic speed in London is
nearly back to that of horse-drawn days. There are special exhibitions focusing on the lively posters and the tradition of good
design that London Transport has been famous for, including one
on Harry Beck's marvellous Underground map. However, the
designer of the 1890 windowless 'Padded Cell' tube carriage took
logic to ridiculous lengths, his argument being that windows were
not required since there was nothing to look at in the tunnels.

Go down the passage between the Museum and the Jubilee
Market, into **Tavistock Street**. On the far side is Hudson House,
built by Edwin Lutyens in 1904 as the offices for the magazine
Country Life, founded a few years before by Edward Hudson. This
was almost Lutyens' first building in London, neo-Georgian overall, though with Baroque detailing, and thumping great chimneys
that recall his Surrey vernacular days of the 1890s. Each ground-
floor window has a cartouche above it with the letters CL and
some carving in the Grinling Gibbons mode. There is also a good
Bedford family coat of arms in stone on the back of the Jubilee
Hall opposite, with their fatalistic (or perhaps insouciant) motto,
'Che sara, sara' – whatever will be, will be.

As you turn right down **Burleigh Street** look at the two corner
buildings: one with carved foliage and flowers, coloured tiles in
the cornice, and fancy brackets; the other with grotesque key-
stones, bearded heads with retroussé noses. Then you will come
on a Victorian vicarage, of all things, squeezed on to an awkward
site. It was built in 1860 by William Butterfield (he of All Saints,
Margaret Street, W1, and Keble College, Oxford) for the long-
demolished church of St Michael, in the polychrome brickwork
that was his speciality.

At the bottom of the street swing right into the **Strand** past the
Strand Palace Hotel in its nasty artificial stone cladding. Its hall

used to have Jazz-Modern decoration by Oliver Bernard (father of Jeffrey and Bruce), but that is now in the Victoria and Albert Museum. Next, past **Exeter Street** where John Evelyn was arrested in 1657 for attending church on Christmas Day, which had been abolished by the Roundheads: 'these were men of high flight and above ordinances, and spake spiteful things of Our Lord's Nativity. As we went up to receive the Sacrament the miscreants held their muskets against us.'

Turn right into **Southampton Street** and your eye will first be caught by the clock designed by Lutyens for the offices of George Newnes, publisher of *Tit-Bits* and *The Strand Magazine*. W. S. Gilbert was born in number 17 and Garrick lived at number 27 from 1750 to 1772. Just below the latter turn left, beneath an onion dome on one side and a conical turret on the other, into **Maiden Lane**. When it was under threat of demolition in the early 1970s, John Betjeman came to its defence: 'Henry James called Warwickshire "unmitigated England" – Maiden Lane is unmitigated London.'

Corpus Christi Roman Catholic church and its attached presbytery make a good Gothic group, yellow brick with yellow and black diaper. One suspects there might be something similar inside, hidden under the white emulsion. **Number 42** opposite is an excellent Gothic, shading into Arts and Crafts, warehouse (1873), and **number 38** is Arts and Crafts of a different breed. Then comes **Rules Restaurant**, founded in 1799 by someone whose identity has vanished, leaving only the name. If you like theatrical and other memorabilia thick on the walls, this is a must. Edward VII, when Prince of Wales, entertained the actress Lillie Langtry in a room upstairs and, more recently, it was Graham Greene's favourite restaurant. Outside it has nice brass cartouches assuring its customers of a 'Recherché table d'hôte'.

On the south side, where the back of the **Vaudeville Theatre** now is, there was a French barber's shop in the eighteenth century called the White Peruque. This was one of the places where **Voltaire** lodged when he was forced into exile in 1726, following a beating administered to him by the servants of the Chevalier de Rohan-Chabot in Paris. Rohan had insulted him earlier and got a cutting retort back. Voltaire stayed in England for three years, perfecting his English by visits to Drury Lane Theatre where he

*The old royal entrance
to the Adelphi Theatre
in Maiden Lane*

Strand amusement arcade

followed the play in a copy borrowed from the prompter. He became an anglophile and incorporated his admiration for English ways and institutions in his *Lettres Philosophiques* which, as much as any book, helped to dissolve the *ancien régime*. Might his admiration have been tempered had he heard of Dryden's treatment by Lord Rochester less than fifty years before (p. 45)?

Later in the century another barber worked in Maiden Lane, at number 21, the father of the painter J. M. W. Turner who was born there in 1775. The basement of this building was a tavern called the Cider Cellar, famous as the haunt of **Richard Porson**, Regius Professor of Greek at Cambridge (1759–1808), one of the greatest classical scholars and a prodigious drinker. His father was a Norfolk worsted weaver, but a patron ensured that Richard got to Eton. Byron saw him in his declining years: 'he used to recite or rather vomit pages of all languages, and could hiccup Greek like a Helot [a Spartan slave]'. Hazlitt also left a memorable vignette of him, in

an old rusty black coat with cobwebs hanging to the skirts of it, and with a large patch of coarse brown paper covering the whole length of his nose, looking for all the world like a drunk carpenter and talking to one of the proprietors [of the London Institution, where he was a very bad librarian] with an air of suavity, approaching to condescension.

In the 1890s **The Adelphi Theatre** was famous for melodramas starring the amiable matinée idol William Terriss. Real life copied art in 1897 when he was stabbed to death by a demented stagehand, just by the royal entrance to the theatre, which can still be seen in Maiden Lane. Ellen Terry said, 'Poor dear Terriss – I do hope he lived long enough to realise he had been murdered. How he would have enjoyed it!' The entrance is next to Fatboy's Diner, an incongruous shiny American caravan which has strayed here from Route 66.

Turn left into **Exchange Court**, one of several alleys running down to the Strand hereabouts, and then right along the Strand until **Zimbabwe House** is reached. This began life as the British Medical Association, built by Charles Holden in 1907 in a free Classical style of much originality. If it appeals, it is also worth seeing his Law Society extension in Chancery Lane. Look at Jacob

Epstein's mutilated statuary on Zimbabwe House in the Strand

The old Charing Cross Hospital, now a police station

Epstein's mutilated statues on the façade, attacked when they were first revealed, threatened again when the Rhodesians took over the building from the doctors, and butchered finally in 1937 on the grounds that their eroded state made them a danger. Look also inside Zimbabwe House, where some of the country's remarkable Shona sculptures should be on display.

Turn up **Agar Street** by the rounded corner of Decimus Burton's old **Charing Cross Hospital** (1834), an harmonious continuation of the style set by John Nash in his Strand block just to the west. **Number 6** Agar Street is a new building echoing Holden's mannerisms and materials; do peer in at its fancy marble reception desk, which could double as a fishmonger's slab. Agar Street ends in Chandos Place, as does this walk. The 'Thank God It's Friday' restaurant to the right is on the site of the blacking factory where the miserable boy Dickens continued to work after it removed here from Hungerford Stairs to the south: 'When I had no money, I took a turn in Covent Garden and stared at the pineapples.' The nearest tube is Charing Cross.

Lutyens' clock in Southampton Street

Charing Cross, the Embankment, Strand, Trafalgar & Leicester Squares

Come up from Charing Cross tube in front of the British Rail station, which has the privilege of being closer to the centre of London than any other. Indeed, all distances to other towns in England used to be measured from Charing Cross. Inside the railings is the replica of the old Cross, the last of the twelve marking the route taken southwards from Lincoln by the body of Edward I's consort, Eleanor of Castile, before final burial in Westminster Abbey in 1292. You will have to go to Northampton or to the village of Geddington in the same county to see what the originals looked like. After the Civil War, in 1647, Parliament had ordered that the cross be dismantled as a superstitious and popish relic. The railway company, with a mix of shrewd promotional instinct and Victorian reverence for the Gothic past, got E. M. Barry, the architect of the Opera House, to run up an approximation to it at the same time as he designed the Charing Cross Hotel, in what John Betjeman called a 'bold, coarse Victorian Renaissance' style. If you arrived via the Northern Line, you will have seen David Gentleman's scenes of the building of the medieval cross in the tube station.

The hotel and the station behind it are built on the site of the Hungerford Market. The Hungerford family, who owned the land hereabouts, suffered as Lancastrians in the Wars of the Roses, revived under Henry VII, but struck a bad patch in the reign of Henry VIII, when the dowager Lady Hungerford was hanged at Tyburn for poisoning her husband, and then her stepson was convicted of treason and sodomy in 1540. Sir Edward Hungerford, the last of the line, was a notorious spendthrift, once blowing 500 guineas on a wig. It was he who in 1678 got an Act of Parliament

The escalator up to Hungerford footbridge from Villiers Street

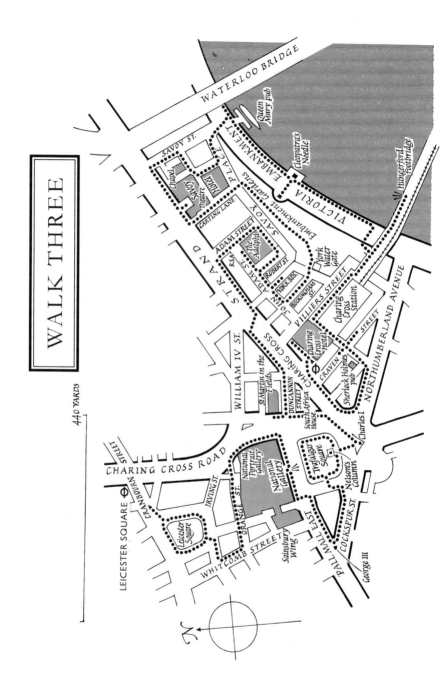

WALK THREE

440 YARDS

WATERLOO BRIDGE

Queen Mary pub

Cleopatra's Needle

Hungerford Footbridge

VICTORIA EMBANKMENT

SAVOY ST.

Chapel

Savoy Theatre

SAVOY

CARTING LANE

FLORAL

ADAM STREET

The Adelphi

RSA

ADAM ST.

ROBERT ST.

YORK BDS.

JOHN ST.

BUCKINGHAM ST.

York Water Gate

Embankment Gardens

STRAND

STRAND

WILLIAM IV ST.

VILLIERS STREET

Charing Cross Station

CHARING CROSS

Charing Cross Hotel

CRAVEN

Sherlock Holmes pub

NORTHUMBERLAND AVENUE

St Martin in the Fields

DUNCANNON STREET

South Africa House

Charles I

STREET

CHARING CROSS ROAD

CRANBOURN STREET

LEICESTER SQUARE

Leicester Square

IRVING ST.

ORANGE ST.

National Portrait Gallery

National Gallery

Trafalgar Square

Nelson's Column

WHITCOMB STREET

Sainsbury Wing

PALL MALL EAST

COCKSPUR ST.

George III

N

entitling him to hold a market . In 1685 Sir Christopher Wren and Sir Stephen Fox (ancestor of Charles James Fox) took the market over, but it was never a success. In 1830 Charles Fowler built a new market, soon linked to the South Bank by a pedestrian suspension bridge designed by Isambard Kingdom Brunel. All was swept away in 1863 by the railway and the only survivors are the chains from Brunel's bridge, re-used to complete his Clifton Suspension Bridge at Bristol.

The hotel was hit by a bomb in the last war and lost its Mansard roofs, which were replaced by the ugly top floor you now see. If you have the time, go inside and mount the main staircase effortlessly thanks to its broad, shallow treads, admiring the cast-iron balustrade as you go. On the first floor you can then have a drink in the 1950s bar with its opulent maple panelling, tea in the 'Rendez-vous lounge', which incorporates the round-topped conservatory above the hotel entrance, or lunch in what Betjeman called 'except for the Ritz, the most finely appointed hotel dining room in London'. The hotel has reciprocated by calling it after him, and has plans to remove the central 'carvery' which will allow the proportions of the whole to speak once more. The Cornish marble columns in the room's corners are particularly noteworthy.

In the 1870s an annexe was built to the east of Villiers Street and linked to the main block by a bridge of sighs, both being refurbished at the moment. The Villiers Street frontage will then get the treatment, which it badly needs. The station itself used to be the gateway to the Continent, and it was from here that Phileas Fogg set out Around the World in Eighty Days. But it long ago lost that glamour; in 1905 it also lost its huge curved roof, which collapsed onto the platforms. In 1915 Admiral 'Jackie' Fisher, took refuge in the Hotel to escape Winston Churchill who, he knew, would otherwise persuade him against his better judgement to allow a final naval attempt on the narrows at Gallipoli.

'I think the full tide of human existence is at Charing Cross,' said Dr Johnson, while Virginia Woolf was prepared to come up to London from Richmond, 'for the sake of hearing the Strand roar'. There is still something of that feeling as the crowds ebb and flow in the Strand towards Trafalgar Square, outside the station. Turn left, and you will shortly be in front of Grand Buildings on the

Charing Cross Hotel's bridge of sighs, spanning Villiers Street

Some of the denizens of the deep carved by Barry Baldwin round the main door of Grand Buildings, Trafalgar Square

corner of the Strand and **Northumberland Avenue**. In 1874 the Duke of Northumberland finally felt he had to sell old Northumberland House, built here in 1603, to the Metropolitan Board of Works, so that a road could be driven through to connect the new Thames Embankment road with Trafalgar Square. All that survives is the glass drawing room, now in the Victoria and Albert Museum, and the statue of the straight-tailed lion of the Percys at their other Thames-side house, at Syon. Northumberland House was in fact built by another great family, the Howards, and only came to the Percys later. In 1637, a Howard daughter married Roger Boyle, the 1st Earl of Orrery; 'the greatest gallant of his time, and the greatest gamester', the poet Sir John Suckling, recorded the scene as if he were a Mummerset rustic:

> At Charing-Crosse, hard by the way
> Where we (thou know'st) do sell our hay,
> There is a house with stairs;
> And there did I see coming down
> Such folk as are not in our town,
> Vorty, at least, in pairs . . .
>
> Her feet beneath her petticoat,
> Like little mice stole in and out,
> As if they feared the light.
> But oh! She dances such a way
> No sun upon an Easter day
> Is half so fine a sight.
>
> Her cheeks so rare a white was on,
> No daisy makes comparison,
> Who sees them is undone;
> For streaks of red were mingled there,
> Such as are on a Katherine pear,
> The side that's next the sun . . .

(The reference in line 2 is to the Haymarket, and the stairs in line 3 are those down to the Thames.)

Grand Buildings are much younger than they seem; indeed the scaffolding poles and building materials on their site provided much of the ammunition of the Poll Tax rioters in March 1990.

The façade is very similar to what it replaced, which began life as the Grand Hotel, one of many erected in the area in the 1870s and 1880s. However, the sculpture by Barry Baldwin with which it is ornamented is quite new and repays close study. Start with the key-stones of the Strand arcade: one winks, one smiles, one sticks out its tongue. Then look at the main entrance. The theme of this is endangered species and there are seventy of them here, as well as Adam and Eve and 'a somewhat disillusioned God-like keystone head . . . the hands of his wristwatch indicating The Eleventh Hour', in the words of the sculptor. Eve has an owl, otter, elephant and fox; Adam, whose bottom is being bitten by the serpent, has an armadillo, a lion, and what Barry Baldwin says is a shape derived from a combination of the human foetus, a mushroom, and the atomic bomb cloud. Under Adam the grouping of the gorilla, giraffe's head, lizard and bat is particularly striking. The lowest panel below Eve includes an alligator, a frog, a dragonfly, and, finally, the sculptor's hammer splashing into a pool.

At the end of the Grand Buildings block turn left into **Craven Passage**, by the Sherlock Holmes pub, which has a tableau of the great detective's room at 221B Baker Street, originally created for the Festival of Britain in 1951 and then acquired by wily brewers who knew a tourist fly-trap when they saw it. Pause as Craven Passage crosses **Craven Street** to look at its unexpected eighteenth-century terraces, already restored at the north end and in process of restoration further down. Its most distinguished inhabitant was **Benjamin Franklin** who arrived at number 36 as agent for the House of Assembly, Philadelphia, in 1757. He was accompanied by his son, who studied law at the Middle Temple, by a servant and by a slave, who soon ran away.

He stayed for many years, the 'unofficial voice of America in London', trying to get the ancestral privileges of the English people accorded to his fellow countrymen. He continued with his enquiries into lightning and electricity, but also invented that for-gotten musical instrument, the glass harmonica. Sometimes known as the musical glasses, it became very fashionable for a spell and Mozart composed for it. Franklin had his eccentricities, such as his 'tonic bath'. This involved sitting in his bedroom 'with-out any clothes whatever . . . either reading or writing'. Sometimes

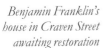

Benjamin Franklin's house in Craven Street awaiting restoration

A cabbies' shelter with its original roof of wooden shingles: Northumberland Avenue

Terry Farrell's space station above Charing Cross

A wine bar in the block where Kipling lodged

he exercised with dumb-bells and sometimes, as he put it, 'Dr Fatsides made 469 turns in his dining room'.

Craven Passage now becomes **The Arches**, which enable you to burrow under Charing Cross Station, and from which you can gain access to the **Players Theatre**, that artificial life-support machine for the late-Victorian music hall. When you emerge from the tunnel, go up the escalator there. This deposits you on an elevated walkway above Villiers Street which goes along the side of **Terry Farrell's** Post-Modern out of High-Tec space station, Embankment Place, built over the railway lines. It has been called 'a monument to the optimism of the 1980s'. On one side, look through the prominent pipework and fancy girders, first at a glass-walled gym full of terrifying machinery – treadmills where executives vainly pursue immortality – and then down at the grandiose granite entrance of the accountants Coopers and Lybrand, whose headquarters this is. On the other side you can look into the windows of Kipling House. Here **Rudyard Kipling** lived when he arrived back from his seven-year apprenticeship on *The Civil and Military Gazette* in Lahore, then in India.

I was so ignorant, I never guessed when the great fogs fell that trains could take me to light and sunshine a few miles outside London. Once I faced the reflection of my own face in the jet-black mirror of the window panes for five days. When the fog thinned, I looked out and saw a man standing opposite . . . Of a sudden his breast turned dull red like a robin's, and he crumpled, having cut his throat. In a few minutes – seconds it seemed – a hand ambulance arrived and took up the body. A pot-boy [from the pub nearby] with a bucket of steaming water sluiced the blood off into the gutter, and what little crowd had collected went its way . . . In Villiers Street I got me an outsize office pewter ink-pot, on which I would gouge the names of the tales and books I wrote out of it. But the housemaids of married life polished those titles away till they grew as faded as a palimpsest.

The walkway turns into **Hungerford Footbridge**, crossing the Thames alongside the ugly bridge carrying the railway lines. Go some way along it for the sake of the view eastwards to the City, St Paul's and Canary Wharf beyond. You can also look back and see Terry Farrell's building as an entity for the first time. There's a flight of steps that will take you down to the entrance to

*Shell–Mex House,
the Adelphi and Terry
Farrell's Embankment
Place, with Cleopatra's
Needle by the Thames*

*One of the
sphinxes flanking
Cleopatra's Needle*

Embankment tube. The buildings here at the foot of Villiers Street and the west end of the Embankment gardens are a real jumble, from the curved Carrara House (1960), through a hideous London Transport erection tacked on the side of the tube entrance, to the good Edwardian baroque of Hungerford House looking over the river, with its lantern and delicate dormers.

The Victoria Embankment, of which the stretch from here to Waterloo Bridge is only a part, was the Metropolitan Board of Works' (p. 33) greatest achievement. It all began with 'The Great Stink' in the dry summer of 1858, when the Thames at Westminster was so smelly, from the raw sewage pouring straight into it, that conditions in the Houses of Parliament became intolerable. Action was demanded and Sir Joseph Bazalgette came up with the plan for a new sewer flowing from west to east into which all the extant sewers could empty themselves, rather than into the river. This huge new *cloaca maxima* would take its contents well to the east of the City, way downstream. By building the Embankment walls close to the low tide mark and then infilling behind, some 37.25 acres in all were created. This made space, not only for the sewer, but also for a road and the new, partially underground, District Railway too. The excavations for the latter provided the subsoil, and the topsoil was brought by barge from Barking Creek, enabling the gardens to be created. The operation was completed in 1870.

By Charing Cross Pier there is a bas-relief memorial to **W. S. Gilbert**, the librettist of Sir Arthur Sullivan's Savoy Operas, by George Frampton. On either side there are seated female figures of Tragedy and Comedy. The latter holds a number of puppet figures including one in Japanese costume, presumably referring to *The Mikado*. There are the distinctive entwined dolphin lamps of the Embankment here, embellished with bearded river gods with reeds in their hair, St Martin cutting his cloak, for the parish of St Martin-in-the-Fields, and the cipher MBW. Complementing them are benches supported at either end by sphinxes. Further east there are also kneeling camel benches, but not here, perhaps out of deference to the Camel Corps memorial on the other side of the road (p. 98).

The dominating feature of this stretch is **Cleopatra's Needle**.

As one of the tablets on it tells us 'This obelisk, prostrate for centuries on the sands of Alexandria, was presented to the British nation in 1819 by Mahommed Ali, Viceroy of Egypt. A worthy memorial of our distinguished countrymen Nelson and Abercromby.' Nelson had destroyed the French fleet at the Battle of the Nile in 1798 and Sir Ralph Abercromby defeated the French Army at Alexandria in 1801. Mahommed Ali owed nominal fealty to the Ottoman sultan in Istanbul, but in reality was quite independent. The Needle, and a twin which is now in Central Park, New York, were first erected by Pharaoh Thothmes III at Heliopolis near Cairo in about 1500 BC. Two hundred years later Rameses the Great added some inscriptions extolling his own victories. Then Cleopatra, over a millennium later, moved them to Alexandria to the memorial she built to her lover Julius Caesar.

The Needle only made it to the Embankment in 1878, and then largely due to the 'patriotic zeal' of a surgeon called Erasmus Wilson. Successful investment in gas and railway shares allowed him to pay £10,000 towards the costs of shipping. The Needle was encased in a cigar-shaped iron hull for the journey, and was nearly lost during a storm in the Bay of Biscay. It had another close call in September 1917 when bombs, from the first raid to which London was subjected by planes rather than Zeppelins, fell nearby. Shrapnel scars can be seen in the granite, and the bronze sphinxes. Notice the ingenious rubbish collector floating in the Thames nearby; the ebbing tide brings the jetsam in, while the flood tide closes the doors and prevents its escape.

Opposite the Needle on the far side of the road is the less-than-entirely successful **Belgian War Memorial**: a mother with a nude young girl and boy, and a lot of swags and garlands (c. 1919). Continue eastwards along the Embankment towards the *Queen Mary*, an old Clyde pleasure steamer retired in 1977 to become a floating pub. If the sight of all the lunchtime joggers from the City gives you a thirst, quench it here. Beyond her is a memorial to **Sir Walter Besant**, one of those admirable, indefatigable Victorian figures, all pince-nez and impenetrable beard: secretary of the Palestine Exploration Fund, founder of the Society of Authors, East End philanthropist. Above is **Waterloo Bridge**, the stumps of its nineteenth-century predecessor still visible below it – the bridge from which Dickens, in his 'Night Walks' essay said,

The river had an awful look, the buildings on the banks were muffled in black shrouds, and the reflected lights seemed to originate deep in the water, as if the spectres of suicides were holding them to show where they went down. The wild moon and clouds were as restless as an evil conscience in a tumbled bed, and the very shadow of the immensity of London seemed to lie oppressively upon the river.

Cross the roads until you are before the statue of **Michael Faraday**, that great electro-chemist and most appealing of scientists. He is in front of what is now the Institute of Electrical Engineers but what was, from 1923 to 1932, Savoy Hill, the headquarters of the British Broadcasting Company, then Corporation. Behind it is the Savoy Chapel, which leads us first into the history of **THE SAVOY** as a whole. For much of its life this area has escaped inclusion in the normal parochial and governmental pattern of London – it was only in 1899 that it became part of Westminster. In 1246 it was given by Henry III to Peter, Count of Savoy, his wife's uncle. By a circuitous route it became the property of Edward III's son, John of Gaunt, only for his splendid palace there to be burnt during the Peasants' Revolt in 1381. Its fortunes eventually revived following the death of Henry VII whose will allowed for the establishment of a large 'hospital', together with a large church and subsidiary chapels. The north, east and west walls of the existing **Savoy Chapel** survive from one of these last. There were dormitories where 100 poor persons were allowed to lodge for one night at a time, complete with hot baths and facilities for delousing clothes. Unfortunately, after the Dissolution of the Monasteries in the 1530s, the hospital lost much of its endowment and thereafter went into a lingering decline.

It was turned into a military hospital in the 1620s, and Dr Henry Killigrew (brother of Thomas of the Drury Lane Theatre, p. 56), who was made Master of the Savoy at the Restoration, failed to return it to its original purposes. His daughter Anne, a poet and painter, was buried in the Savoy Chapel in 1685. Her death inspired Dryden to write what Dr Johnson called the noblest ode in the English language. It is hard to agree with that, but the poem does have its moments:

O wretched we! Why were we hurried down
This lubric and adult'rate age,
(Nay, added fat pollutions of our own)
T'increase the steaming ordures of the stage?

When in mid-air the golden trump shall sound,
To raise the nations under ground;
When in the valleys of Jehoshaphat
The judging God shall close the book of fate,
And there the last assizes keep
For those who wake and those who sleep;
When rattling bones together fly
From the four corners of the sky . . .

The area's peculiar status attracted the lawless and debtors. In 1696 a tailor who tried to demand payment there was tarred and feathered, then tied to the maypole in the Strand. By then, some of the buildings had become a barracks for the Foot Guards. In the mid-eighteenth century, the chaplain made a large income from performing illicit marriages, until the law caught up with him. In 1776 there was a big fire but it was forty years before redevelopment began. In 1820 the architect Robert Smirke built the south wall of the Chapel and moved the tower to its present position. In 1864 the Chapel was burnt and only the walls were left standing.

It is often assumed that it is a Chapel Royal, but this is incorrect: it is 'the private chapel of the sovereign in the right of the Duchy of Lancaster, free and exempt from all ecclesiastical juristiction'. In the 1880s it became very fashionable for weddings and it was then that its musical tradition was really founded. In 1937 it became the chapel of the Royal Victorian Order.

Continue past the green graveyard up the surprisingly steep hill to the Strand, when you can behave like Vesta Tilley:

I'm Burlington Bertie,
I rise at ten-thirty
And saunter along like a toff.
I walk down the Strand
With my gloves on each hand,
And I walk back again with them off.

The Savoy Chapel with part of the Savoy Hotel behind

The ornate entrance to Savoy Buildings off the Strand, with Piranesian scaffolding beyond

The first watering hole on the south side is **Simpson's**, at 100 Strand. It is a temple to the glorification of the roast: roast beef, lamb, duck, chicken. (It used, of course, to be mutton, not lamb.) Having started, perhaps, with potted shrimps, and moved steadily through the roast, those who still have a corner to fill up settle for treacle roll accompanied by a sauceboat of custard. If you can eat two helpings, Simpson's offer a third free. The place opened in 1828 as the Grand Cigar Divan. It soon became recognised as the home of English chess, and the chess theme was maintained in some of the decorations when it was rebuilt by Thomas Collcutt about the turn of the century. Until 1984 women were not allowed to eat downstairs; and in the basement, a continuous spittoon runs round the foot of the bar. The loins of beef and saddles of lamb are wheeled from table to table on trolleys equipped with silver lids to keep the meat warm, and your portion is carved for you with panache and generosity. Some of the trolleys date back to the days of John Simpson, in the 1850s.

Almost immediately after Simpson's comes the turn into the forecourt of **The Savoy Theatre** and Hotel, the only place in Britain where you drive on the right. The theatre was built by Richard D'Oyly Carte, the impresario behind Gilbert and Sullivan's operas, and opened in 1881. This team had a string of successes, until the cantankerous Gilbert fell out with D'Oyly Carte over the cost of carpeting the foyer in 1890. In 1929 the interior was redecorated in Art Deco style, which still remains, having been carefully restored after a fire in 1990.

Two or three years after the theatre opened, D'Oyly Carte decided to plough some of the profits into a hotel nearby. In 1889 the **SAVOY HOTEL** was finished complete with 'ascending rooms' (lifts), full electric light and no fewer than sixty-seven bathrooms, a huge number for the time. Its ground plan is confusing, partly because it was built in two stages, and partly because of its steeply sloping site. The lower, river, block was the earliest, followed in 1904 by that fronting on to the Strand. The architect of both was Thomas Collcutt, who also built the magnificent Palace Theatre for D'Oyly Carte at Cambridge Circus. It was the river block, with César Ritz as manager and Auguste Escoffier as *maître chef*, that established the hotel's name. In March 1893 Oscar Wilde

The Strand entrance to the Savoy

The inconsolable mourner below Sir Arthur Sullivan's memorial bust in Embankment Gardens

wrote to Lord Alfred Douglas from the Savoy, 'My bill here is £49 for a week. I have also got a new sitting room overlooking the Thames . . . I fear I must leave; no money, no credit, and a heart of lead.' In his extended letter to Douglas, known as *De Profundis*, written from Reading gaol in 1897, he filled in the details:

The Savoy dinners – the clear turtle soup, the luscious ortolans wrapped in their crinkled Sicilian vine-leaves, the heavy amber-coloured, indeed almost amber-scented champagne – Dagonet 1880, I think, was your favourite wine? – all have to be paid for.

The Savoy kitchens collected another literary accolade some time later when an omelette made with smoked haddock was created for Arnold Bennett.

In 1899 Claude Monet the painter stayed at the Savoy for six weeks, in a room on the sixth floor of the river block, and came back again in the following two years. He had already done some famous series of paintings – of haystacks, poplars, the west front of Rouen Cathedral – but here he produced the biggest yet, seeking to catch the Thames bridges and the Houses of Parliament in every mood of atmosphere and light. Such was the constant variation that by nine in the morning he had often worked on five different canvases. More recently Oscar Kokoschka was also fascinated by the same sweep of the river as it alters course through ninety degrees.

The Savoy's River Restaurant is a favourite location for power breakfasts, or even just to share Monet's view. The Grill (yew panelling, no view) is the place for power lunches, on the left underneath the Strand entrance awning that looks like the top of a Rolls Royce radiator. (However, it has a shiny statue of the Count of Savoy on top rather than a winged lady.) The Thames Foyer, where Cecil Beaton's original pleated silk has been transformed into more permanent plaster, is for tea; then you can progress to the American Bar before gravitating to the Ballroom, created out of the former stable yard. Here Gershwin gave the first British performance of his *Rhapsody in Blue*, in spite of the Savoy being famous for its pink table linen. When it is time for bed you will sleep on a mattress made by the Savoy Group's own craftsmen, and be able to summon a maid or valet stationed on each floor by ringing one of the bells (there is even one by the bath). To recover from all the excess there are now a swimming pool and gym, created above the Theatre after the 1990 fire.

As you emerge into the Strand once more, look at the startling green roof of the 1904 block and at the figures seated underneath the eaves, with the facing of Doulton's Carrara ware – matt cream terracotta – below. Then spare a glance for the **Savoy Tailors' Guild** shop on the corner, with its delicately carved wood window surrounds, brass columns and period interior. It is also worth sticking your head into the courtyard of **Shell-Mex House** a little further west along the Strand. This was once the Hotel Cecil, a rival of the Savoy, but the Embankment block was rebuilt by Shell in Art Deco white stonework; the contrast between it and the Strand frontage is arresting. In the 1930s some of the best and brightest writers and artists were employed or commissioned here by the Shell advertising department, including John Piper, Graham Sutherland, Rex Whistler and John Betjeman.

Go back down the steps into Carting Lane, which will take you into **Victoria Embankment Gardens**, just by the river entrance to the Savoy with its incongruous 1950s Festival of Britain-type porte cochère. If you look up at either the west or east side of this oldest part of the hotel, you can see some of the original Arts and Crafts metal bas-reliefs of Muses, together with metal foliage balustrades. The Gardens have a sizeable population of statues, by far and away the best of which is the memorial to **Sir Arthur Sullivan** by Goscombe John. His bust stares towards the Hotel, pretending to be unaware that draped around the plinth supporting it is the most erotic sculpture of a woman in London, so nominated in a poll carried out by the *Evening Standard* a few years ago. Distinctly underdressed for the English climate, she raises the ambient temperature several degrees even on the most dank and dripping morning, and in spite of the statue to Robert Raikes, founder of the Sunday School movement, being her closest neighbour.

At this end there are memorials to Henry Fawcett (d. 1884), the radical Liberal MP, and (by Lutyens) to Lord Cheylesmore – a forgotten figure, but in his day Grenadier Guardsman, Major-General, Mayor of Westminster and Chairman of the L.C.C. Fawcett was blinded in a shooting accident but this did not prevent him from championing the causes of women's rights and of open spaces. He also has an excellent memorial in Westminster Abbey, by Alfred Gilbert.

While walking westwards through the Gardens, one should take in the curving sweep of large buildings stretching from Waterloo Bridge to Hungerford Bridge, which can be appreciated from here. Whatever their individual defects, they have a presence when seen as a group, at a distance. The 1930s Brettenham House is the most easterly, followed by the Savoy, refaced in artificial stone in 1910. Then comes Shell-Mex House with its Art Deco clock, flanked by four robed figures with bowed heads; its only other decoration is some very stylised eagles. Compared to Shell's other headquarters building, all too visible on the South Bank just beyond Hungerford Bridge, it is a work of genius. The central Adelphi block (1936–38) is normally cast as one of London's architectural villains, but distance, if it does not lend enchantment, does flatter its sculpture and Art Deco detailing, and allows it to play a part in the sequence. Terry Farrell's building over Charing Cross station rounds things off.

Passing the catalpa tree planted in the Coronation year of 1953, which is doing very well, you will come on more statuary. **Sir Wilfrid Lawson** (d. 1906) was another radical Liberal MP. His two causes were prohibition and anti-imperialism – 'Little Englander' was a phrase he invented. 'We raise £30m by killing our people with alcohol; and expend the same on gunpowder to kill people abroad.' But he was no killjoy, buying John Peel's pack of foxhounds in Cumberland and acting as something of a court jester in the Commons. In 1979 four small figures from his plinth were stolen. The statue of **Robert Burns**, among London's ugliest, is a smaller replica of that in Central Park, New York, for which one must be profoundly grateful. The eye is mesmerised by the hobnails on the soles of his shoes, which appear to be laced up with worms. It is a relief to turn to the almost dainty camel and rider of the memorial to the First World War **Imperial Camel Corps**, by far the greatest number of whom seem to have been Australians.

This end of the Gardens degenerates into a clutter of buildings: bandstand, tea house, gardeners' depot, lavatories. Turn instead towards the **York Water Gate**. York House here had been given to the Archbishop of York by Queen Mary in 1556, but by 1624 it belonged to George Villiers, Duke of Buckingham and favourite of James I and Charles I. He seems only to have used it on such occasions as that in 1625 when he entertained 'all the Ambassadors and all the French' at the marriage celebrations of Charles I and Henrietta Maria of France: 'such magnificence and prodigal plenty, both for curious cheer and banquet . . . hath not been seen nor known in these parts. One rare dish came by mere chance: a sturgeon of full six foot long that afternoon not far from the place, leaping into a sculler's boat, was served in at supper' (*The Chamberlain Letters*). This river entrance was constructed in 1626 to create a suitable first impression on his arriving guests. The designer is unknown; it might be Inigo Jones, though the sculptor Nicholas Stone, and an artistic 'fixer' of the day called Balthasar Gerbier are also mentioned. Whoever it was, he had as model the Fontaine de Médicis at the Luxembourg Palace in Paris. The decoration is all to the greater glory of Buckingham, with the anchors on shields supported by lions referring to his office of Lord High Admiral. Shells echo those on the Cross in the Villiers coat of arms, which impale those of the Manners family, Earls of Rutland, on the north side of the Gate. The Villiers motto is also there: *Fidei Coticula Crux* – the Touchstone of Faith is the Cross.

The 2nd Duke of Buckingham forfeited York House in the Civil War and it came into the possession of Thomas, Lord Fairfax, the Parliamentary commander. However, the duke got it back by marrying Fairfax's daughter, whose tutor had been Andrew Marvell (p. 12); it would be good to have his comment on the match. After 1660, Buckingham outdid even Lord Rochester in debauchery and by 1672 York House had been sold to three speculators for development. One of them was the notorious Nicholas Barbon, who appears so often in the Inns of Court volume in this series. Another was Anthony Deane, the great shipbuilder and friend of Samuel Pepys. In 1679, at the height of the Popish Plot scare (pp. 13 and 16), Deane and Pepys were accused of 'Piracy, Popery and Treachery' and committed to the Tower. One of the leaders of the clique who levelled the false accusations was Buckingham. But the tables were turned before long. Buckingham was to die 'worn to a thread with whoring', as Pope unforgettably described:

> In the worst inn's worst room, with mat half-hung,
> The floor of plaster and the walls of dung,
> On once a flock-bed, but repaired with straw,
> With tape-tied curtains, never meant to draw,
> The George and Garter dangling from that bed,
> Where tawdry yellow strove with dirty red . . .

Pepys and Deane were released in spite of the fact that, as Sir Roger Lestrange (p. 13) put it, 'Cases in those days were carried by huzzas instead of votes, and bear-garden law was all many an honest man had to trust to for the liberty of the subject.' Pepys went to stay with his clerk Will Hewer who was living at number 12 **Buckingham Street**, just to the north of the York Water Gate, one of the new houses built on Buckingham's former property. Pepys later took the house over from Hewer and, in the free-and-easy way of those days, was allowed to transfer the Admiralty Office there when he was once more Secretary of it. In April 1687 John Evelyn was entertained by Pepys at number 12 and

heard the famous singer Cifaccio, esteemed the best in Europe. Indeed his holding out and delicateness in extending and looseing a note with incomparable softnesse and sweetnesse were admirable; for the rest I found him a mere wanton, effeminate child, very coy, and proudly conceited to my apprehension. He touch'd the harpsichord to his voice rarely well.

In 1688 Pepys moved to number 14, and when he retired to Clapham it was taken by Robert Harley, Earl of Oxford, in effect Queen Anne's Prime Minister, who entertained Jonathan Swift there. In the early nineteenth century it was the home of artists: William Etty, whose nudes Queen Victoria bought, and Clarkson Stanfield (p. 57).

Number 22 at the north-east end is a Victorian cuckoo in Buckingham Street's nest of seventeenth- and eighteenth-century houses. It was the office of a leading architect of the high Gothic revival, William Burges, and indeed had been designed by his brother-in-law R. P. Pullan. It has an elaborate porch with ivy-leaf

of Alley, the last trace

*Sunday morning,
Buckingham Street*

The York Water Gate

capitals, and a fancy frieze of coloured tiles under the eaves. Burges must have felt very much at ease, given his penchant for the oddball and colourful as displayed in his work at Cardiff Castle and Castel Coch. Coleridge lodged at number 21 in the winter of 1799–1800 after coming back from his first tour of the Lake District with Wordsworth. He had overspent his allowance from the Wedgwood family and needed to earn money from journalism, so wrote seventy-six articles for the *Morning Post*.

The street names hereabouts used to include 'George', 'Villiers', 'Duke', 'of', and 'Buckingham'. Alas, of Alley has become York Place. To the east, it is the Adam family that monopolises the street signs. William Adam was a successful Scottish architect and three of his sons, Robert, James and John, followed in his footsteps. Robert was very much the leader of the pack, taking himself off on an elaborate Grand Tour of Italy which culminated in a trip to the ruins of the Emperor Diocletian's palace at Spalatro (Split) on the Dalmatian coast opposite. His lavish folio on the ruins, published in 1764, and his appointment as architect to George III two years before, were the keys with which he gained access to the plum jobs in Britain's stately homes. His early commissions included Kedleston in Derbyshire, Harewood in Yorkshire and Syon opposite Kew.

These successes emboldened the brothers to take the lease of the site of the former Durham House below the Strand here in 1768, from Nell Gwynn's descendant, the Duke of St Albans. The plan was to embank the Thames for the first time, build an arcade next to it, leading to the vaults, which would support a terrace above, on which a complex of houses was to be built. The whole was to be called the **ADELPHI**, from the Greek for brothers. It was an ambitious speculation, based on the expectation that the Ordnance Department would rent the vaults. This never came about and it proved more difficult to sell the houses than expected, in spite of the lead given by David Garrick, who took one in the central block. To avoid bankruptcy a lottery, with houses as prizes, had to be promoted.

What is left is only a fraction of the original, but there is enough to make one bitterly regret the loss of the rest, which took place in two stages. First the main blocks were covered in Portland cement and given 'Italianate' additions in 1872; then they were demolished in 1936. Go to the south end of Robert Street and the junction of John Adam with Adam Street to see what has been lost. Those elegant door frames, surprisingly solid-looking wrought-iron balconies and railings, and pilasters with formalised honeysuckle climbing up them, as it were, all speak of one of the happiest moments in English urban architecture. Horace Walpole may have sneered at the last element when he wrote of 'warehouses, laced down the seams, like a soldier's frill in a regimental old coat', but he was only phrasemaking, not using his eyes. More of the wrought ironwork, with its heart-and-honeysuckle motif echoing the pilaster decoration, can be seen in the ironwork gallery, and on the walls above the shop, at the Victoria and Albert Museum. And some of the curved vaulting supporting the terrace can be viewed by entering **Lower Robert Street**, off York Buildings, at the western end of the Adelphi. It is a misnomer to call it a street since in reality it is a cobbled tunnel.

Of the eighteenth-century inhabitants of the Adelphi, **David Garrick** must be the most outstanding, holding his weekly sauerkraut parties for his distinguished friends. When he died here, Johnson awarded him one of the greatest of all epitaphs: 'His death eclipsed the gaiety of nations, and diminished the public stock of harmless pleasure.' Such could most definitely not be said about a certain **Dr Graham** who established a 'Temple of Health' at the Adelphi in 1780. This quack adorned his hall with crutches, ear trumpets and spectacles which he claimed belonged to those he had cured. In the rooms above were electrical machines, glass globes, statues, carved dragons, stained glass, incense and his 'celestial bed'. A night of procreation in this last, he claimed, ensured beautiful progeny, and he charged accordingly. Nelson's mistress, Emma Hamilton, was said to have posed in the nude here, in her early days, as an attraction or stimulus. This story is probably what the Italians call 'ben trovato'. The doctor was too good to last and, after opium addiction followed by religious enthusiasm, he died a lunatic, in Edinburgh.

Richard Arkwright, inventor of the Spinning Jenny, lived at number 8 Adam Street. Dr Johnson was said to have been the only man who saw its importance at once, without explanation.

The central Adelphi block

*A surviving fragment of
Robert Adam's Adelphi,
Robert Street*

In the nineteenth century **William Butterfield**, another highly original Gothic revivalist like William Burges (p. 101), had his offices at numbers 4 and 5 (p. 72). **Sir Arthur Blomfield**, an accomplished but more eclectic Victorian architect, also had his offices at the Adelphi, and in them worked the novelist **Thomas Hardy**. He recalled that 'the rooms contained fine Adam mantel-pieces in white marble on which we used to sketch caricatures in pencil'.

The northern part of the Adelphi site is occupied by the **ROYAL SOCIETY OF ARTS**, which commissioned the building it still occupies from Robert Adam in 1771. The RSA was founded in 1754 by William Shipley, a drawing master from Northampton, 'for the encouragement of Arts, Manufactures and Commerce'. This it still does in a multitude of different ways, through its lectures, publications and projects in business, industry, education, design and the environment. In the 1770s its Great Room, as well as being used for lectures, was the scene of the annual prize-giving for inventions and works of art submitted to the Society. By telephoning in advance (0171 930 5115) it is possible to be shown this. It is well worth doing so because it is decorated with one of the most ambitious yet bizarre series of paintings in the country, which allow one to forget its raked cinema seating. Adam's impressive brick vaults beneath the RSA have now been restored and turned into dining and conference rooms; ask to see these too.

James Barry, an Irishman, was the wild man of British painting, proud, quarrelsome and impoverished. In 1777 he offered to decorate the Great Room at no cost to the Society, in his own words, 'to illustrate one great maxim or moral truth, that the obtaining of happiness, as well individual as public, depends on cultivating the human faculties'. The first scene is of 'Orpheus . . . and the hearers of Orpheus . . . clad in the spoils of wild beasts'. Then follows 'a Grecian Harvest-Home . . . a state of happiness, simplicity and fecundity . . . though not attended with much éclat.' The third is 'Crowning the Victors at Olympia', then comes 'Commerce, or the Triumph of the Thames . . . If some of those mermaids appear more sportive than industrious, and others still more wanton than sportive, the picture has variety and, I am sorry to add, the greater resemblance to the truth.' In the 'Distribution of Premiums in the Society of Arts', Barry has portrayed a great many distinguished contemporary figures. The last scene is 'Elysium, or the State of Final Retribution', with some marvellous juxtapositions of figures from history: 'Alfred the Great . . . is leaning on the shoulder of William Penn . . . Just over the Black Prince and Peter the Great, I have brought together Swift, Erasmus and Cervantes.' Among the damned is 'an enraged King who lived in times prior to the actual and understood limitations of monarchy.'

Emerge into the Strand once more and cross to number 440 on its far side, the headquarters building of **Coutts**, bankers to the Queen. Their glass front intrudes in the middle of Nash's West Strand Improvements, planned in 1830, with his distinctive pepper-pots at each corner. This was part of a masterly scheme, which included the creation of Trafalgar Square, its linkage with Lower Regent Street via Pall Mall East, and with the British Museum to the north by a road, which never got built. Thomas Coutts has already been encountered because of his marriage to Harriot Mellon, the actress (p. 51). His brother James (p. 41) first travelled south from Edinburgh, where their father had been Lord Provost, and became partner in an extant bank; Thomas then joined him. Until 1904 the bank was hereabouts, but on the south side of the Strand. If you peer through the glass you will see Thomas in marble at the top of the escalator.

Go now to **St Martin-in-the-Fields**, the fourth church on the site, completed by James Gibbs in 1726. The Baroque infection that Gibbs had acquired during his student days in Rome, and which is clearly detectable in his St Mary-le-Strand (1717), had left him by the time he designed this entirely classical exercise. So it is ironic that the church now prides itself on being London's biggest centre for Baroque music, with frequent evening concerts, and free ones, at lunchtime. The only architectural aspect at which we are meant to look askance is the positioning of the tower, emerging as it does mid-roof, rather than at the west end. Inside, box pews survive in the aisles and at the back. On either side of the altar at gallery level are the 'Royal Box' and the 'Admiralty Box'. George I, whose arms adorn the pediment, was the first churchwarden. There is an ugly blue stained-glass cross in the east window, but the two pink cherubs blowing trumpets on top of the new (1990) organ make up for it.

In 1914 the church acquired a new vicar, Dick Sheppard. He got rid of locked private pews belonging to rich families from St James's Square and Carlton House Terrace, opened the crypt and began the tradition of ministering to the homeless that continues strongly today. Perhaps he was inspired in part by one of Dickens' encounters, described in 'Night Walks':

I came to the great steps of St Martin's church as the clock was striking Three. Suddenly, a thing that in a moment more I should have trodden upon without seeing, rose up at my feet with a cry of loneliness and houselessness, struck out of it by the bell, the like of which I have never heard. We then stood face to face looking at one another, frightened by one another. The creature was like a beetle-browed hare-lipped youth of twenty, and it had a loose bundle of rags on, which it held together with one of its hands. It shivered from head to foot, and its teeth chattered, and as it stared at me – persecutor, devil, ghost, whatever it thought me – it made with its whining mouth as if it were snapping at me, like a worried dog. Intending to give this ugly object money, I put out my hand to stay it – for it recoiled as it whined and snapped – and laid my hand upon its shoulder. Instantly, it twisted out of its garment, like the young man in the New Testament, and left me standing alone with its rags in my hands.

Just because you neither want to rub brasses nor drink coffee, do not avoid the **Crypt**. It has good brick vaulting and a couple of outstanding seventeenth-century epitaphs tucked away. Mrs Elizabeth Macdonald died in 1670, 'The well coucht abstract of her creed . . . Thund [tuned] to heaven where now she sings/Anthems to the King of Kings.' Frances Jones, on the other hand, died in 1672, young and unmarried:

> Courtship, which living, she declin'd,
> When dead, to offer, were unkind . . .
> Nor can the truest wit or friend,
> Without detracting, her commend,
> To say she lived a virgin chaste
> In this age loose and all unlaced.

To the north of the church is Nash's **St Martin's National School**, a most dignified composition of round-headed windows,

Ionic pilasters and rustication (c. 1830). South of the church is **South Africa House** by Sir Herbert Baker. Its best features are its south-west corner with a rounded screen of columns, and various animal keystones – buffalo, antelope, elephant and giraffe. With those on Grand Buildings (p. 84), they make this area something of a stone menagerie. Earlier this was the site of the famous coaching inn, the Golden Cross. In his piece 'Early Coaches' from *Sketches By Boz*, Dickens gives an anything-but-romantic picture of this form of travel:

The cold sleet is drizzling down with that gentle regularity, which betokens a duration of four-and-twenty hours at least . . . It strikes a quarter past five as you trudge down Waterloo Place on your way to the Golden Cross and you discover, for the first time, that you were called an hour too early . . . You arrive at the office, and look wistfully up the yard for the Birmingham High-flier, which, for aught you can see, may have flown away altogether, for no preparations appear to be on foot for the departure of any vehicle in the shape of a coach. You wander into the booking-office, which with the gas-lights and blazing fire, looks quite comfortable by contrast . . . There stands the book-keeper. As he informs you, that the coach is up the yard, and will be brought round in about a quarter of an hour, you leave your bag, and repair to 'The Tap' – not with any absurd idea of warming yourself, because you feel such a result to be utterly hopeless, but for the purpose of procuring some hot brandy-and-water, which you do – when the kettle boils! an event which occurs exactly two minutes and a half before the time fixed for the starting of the coach.

  The first stroke of six peals from St Martin's church steeple just as you take the first sip of the boiling liquid. You find yourself at the booking-office in two seconds, and the tap-waiter finds himself much comforted by your brandy-and-water, in about the same period. The coach is out: the horses are in, and the guard and two or three porters are stowing the luggage away, and running up the steps of the booking-office, and down the steps of the booking-office with breathless rapidity. . . . 'Take off the cloths, Bob,' says the coachman . . . 'Now, gen'lm'n,' cries the guard, with the waybill in his hand. 'Five minutes behind time already!' . . . 'Let 'em go, Harry. Give 'em their heads,' cries the coachman – and off we start.

On a triangular island south of Nelson's column, on the spot where the original Charing Cross stood until 1647, there now stands Le Soeur's equestrian **Statue of Charles I**, looking down Whitehall to the Banqueting House where he was executed in 1649. Le Soeur was a man of great conceit who took to signing himself Praxiteles Le Soeur without much justification, as this statue shows. The King's face is bland and unmodelled and his charger, though very well hung underneath, looks like an inflated sausage skin. The contract for the statue said the King's figure should be 'proportionate six foot'. Charles was actually only five foot, four – a little taller than Nelson. Erosion of the carved stonework of the plinth has produced a bizarre textured effect. For a stunning vision of Charles on horseback, wait for the painting by Van Dyck in the National Gallery.

Charles' Lord Treasurer, Richard Weston, commissioned the statue for his country estate in the 1630s. At some point in the Civil War it was bought by the parish of St Paul's, Covent Garden, and erected in the churchyard there. After the King's death it was taken down and at the Restoration a brazier in Holborn produced it, claiming he had bought it from the parish and then preserved it throughout Cromwell's rule, at great risk. In 1675 Charles II bought it from the Weston family and it was erected here, on the site where a number of those who had signed his father's death warrant were executed in 1660. In October of that year Pepys watched Major-General Harrison being hanged, drawn and quartered here, 'he looking as cheerful as any man could do in that condition'. Since 1893, the Royal Stuart Society has laid a wreath here every year on 30 January, the date of the king's execution. There is also an elaborate triple lamp standard on the island, dated 1878, with winged and fish-tailed lions at the base and three putti with linked arms above.

Although **TRAFALGAR SQUARE** was conceived by John Nash (p. 106), it was executed by Sir Charles Barry. Its sloping site made it tricky to handle and Barry's solution was the terrace to the north, with steps leading down from it. The clearance which preceded the layout allowed the west front of St Martin's to be viewed properly for the first time. How marvellous it would be if the road in front of the National Gallery could be buried so that one could walk across to the central area without braving the traffic. Thomas Railton's design for the actual Nelson memorial was selected from

Trafalgar Square: one of Landseer's lions with Nelson at Copenhagen behind

Eroded sculpture on the plinth of the equestrian statue of Charles I

General Sir Charles Napier

124 submitted. The column itself is Devon granite, the Corinthian capital is bronze cast at Woolwich from melted-down cannon, while Nelson is carved from stone. The four bas-reliefs, all by different sculptors, illustrate Nelson's greatest moments. That to the west shows him at the end of the Battle of Cape St Vincent in 1797, accepting, 'extravagant as it may seem . . . the swords of the vanquished Spaniards, which as I received I gave to William Fearney, one of my bargemen, who placed them with the greatest sang-froid, under his arm.' On the north, Nelson is seen wounded at the Battle of the Nile in 1798, on the east at Copenhagen in 1801. This scene, showing Nelson sealing his letter to go with a flag of truce to the Danish Crown Prince, is inaccurate because the incident took place below decks:

The letter being written and carefully folded, he sent for a stick of sealing wax: the person dispatched for the wax had his head taken off by a cannonball: which fact being reported to the admiral, he merely said, 'Send another messenger for the wax.' . . . It was done, and the letter sealed . . . 'Had I made use of a wafer,' said Nelson, 'the wafer would have been still wet when the letter was presented to the Crown Prince: he would have inferred that the letter was sent off in a hurry: and that we had some very pressing reasons for being in a hurry. The wax told no tales.'

The southern bas-relief shows Nelson mortally wounded at Trafalgar in 1805. The final element is Landseer's four lions, supposedly all cast from a single original, although their tails alternate on the right and left of the bodies. A Chinese-language newspaper in Hong Kong has lately paid for the column, the lions, bas-reliefs, other statues in the square, and the fountains to be floodlit.

The nautical note continues northward where there are two basins designed by Lutyens (1939), with mermaid and mermen fountains in them. These zestful figures have double tails and are either seated astride a dolphin and holding porpoises, or in a large scallop shell. The mermen are by Sir Charles Wheeler and the mermaids by W. McMillan (1948). These are really London's only decent fountains, and have the added purpose of helping crowd control by preventing too large an unbroken body of people from assembling at what has become the country's most famous political rallying point. Witness the mixed Socialist and Irish radical rally on 'Bloody Sunday', 13 November 1887 and the Poll Tax riots in March 1990.

There are the busts of three admirals from this century against the north wall: **Jellicoe**, called by Churchill 'the only man who could lose the [first] war in an afternoon'; **Beatty**, 'There is something wrong with our bloody ships today'; and **Cunningham** from the Second World War. Also located here are the Imperial Standards of Length (at 62 °Fahrenheit) installed by the Board of Trade in 1876: 1 ft, 2 ft, 1 yd, 100 ft; a standard chain of 100 links making 66 ft (22 yds, or a cricket pitch); a rod, pole or perch of 5½ yds. Where better for such a defiant stand against creeping metrication? The north-east corner of the square has an equestrian statue of **George IV** riding bare-back and stirrupless, by Chantrey. It was originally intended for the top of Marble Arch, when it was located in front of Buckingham Palace, but ended up here in 1843. A matching plinth at the north-west corner has always been empty. It must ideally have an equestrian statue, which presents a problem to the committee with the task of now finding a candidate.

There used to be a statue of General Gordon between the two basins, but he was removed to make room for the temporary exhibition of a Lancaster bomber in 1943 and is now on the Embankment. (Edward Jenner, in Kensington Gardens, was also once here.) However, Generals Napier and Havelock still flank Nelson's column. **Sir Charles Napier** fought ferociously and was much wounded during the Peninsular War. In the early 1840s he was sent to India where he conquered Sind against ridiculous odds, and either did or didn't send the news home in the form of a dreadful pun, the one Latin word 'Peccavi' – I have sinned. Always a champion of the oppressed, he was a brilliant administrator as well as commander, and Sir Robert Peel said he was a better writer than his brother William Napier, the historian of the Peninsular War. The amazing nose on the face of his statue is no exaggeration. **Sir Henry Havelock** made his name in India too when, after long years of service there, he turned the tide of the Indian Mutiny in 1857, by relieving Lucknow, and then died shortly afterwards. His earnest evangelical Christianity made him particularly appealing to the mid Victorians.

The only other inhabitants of the square are the horrible **pigeons**. It costs Westminster Council £50,000 a year to fight a losing battle against their droppings, but no doubt there would be an outcry if they were killed off. The article in *Oz* magazine all those years ago that provoked the biggest protest post bag was on how to stalk, kill and cook a Trafalgar Square pigeon. One practical suggestion: move the pigeon-feed concession from its nasty hut to the obsolete police phone kiosk at the south-east corner, which at present only houses some brooms.

Canada House on the west side of the square was built in 1827 by Sir Robert Smirke for the Royal College of Physicians and the Union Club. The Physicians got a grand Ionic portico on the north side to rival that erected by the Surgeons on their headquarters in Lincoln's Inn Fields. The Canadians are soon to move out and there should be a good row over what institution or collection takes their place. Beyond it is the equestrian statue of **George III** by Matthew Cotes Wyatt (1836), glaring at New Zealand House at the foot of the Haymarket. The original plan was for the king to be portrayed in a toga driving a chariot, but luckily the money subscribed did not run to that, so we are left with the 'Pigtail and Pump Handle' – the handle being the horse's tail. Swiftly on to another much better royal statue, of **James II** (1686), pointing with his baton at the pedestrian crossing outside the National Gallery. He is in scaly Roman armour and kilt with a laurel wreath on his head, and was at various other London locations before arriving here after the last war. This and a similar one of Charles II at Chelsea Hospital were commissioned, probably from Arnold Quellin, by Tobias Rustat, a senior royal servant, 'a very simple, ignorant but honest and loyal creature'. Beyond it is a replica of Houdon's famous marble statue of **George Washington** at Richmond, Virginia. He is in the act of retiring, a walking stick in his hand and his sword hung up. There is a plough ready for him behind. The thirteen staves round the pillar stand for the then number of states in the Union, and are interspersed with Red Indian arrows. If George III knew he was so close, he would fall off his horse. Both James II and Washington have a very effective fig hedge behind them.

Two London institutions owe a great deal to an expatriate

Russian banker called John Julius Angerstein, who died in 1823. He, as much as anyone, was responsible for the pre-eminence of Lloyds in the world insurance market, and his distinguished collection of pictures, when auctioned in 1824, was bought by the government to form the basis of a national collection of art. In the following decade William Wilkins built the **NATIONAL GALLERY** to house the collection, on the site of what had been the Royal Mews. His effort has never been regarded as a great success and quickly earned the sobriquet of the National Cruet Stand, with its mustard-pot cupola and pepper-caster campaniles. Certainly not impressive seen head on, it is much improved if viewed at an angle from Pall Mall East or Duncannon Street. Wilkins was required to incorporate some of the bases and capitals from the columns of George IV's Carlton House, demolished in 1829, which perhaps helped cramp his style.

Since the opening of the Sainsbury Wing at the west end, there has been a choice of entrances from Trafalgar Square. Let us be old fashioned and go up the steps and in under Wilkins' portico, pausing there for one of London's best views, back over the square and down Whitehall. Spare a glance for the ladies above the door perched on a horse and a camel, and the capitals encased in hairnets to keep the cursed pigeons off. Immediately inside the doors the ceilings are unpleasantly low and covered in rough, abrasive-looking plaster, but things quickly improve. Before feasting your eyes on conventional paintings, look down at the floors of the various vestibules and the half-landing of the grand staircase here, which are covered by a series of **mosaics** as ambitious as those by Eduardo Paolozzi at Tottenham Court Road tube (p. 8). They are all by the Russian-born Boris Anrep who worked on them between 1928 and 1952. As can be deduced from the personalities appearing in them, he was well acquainted with the Bloomsbury Group: Virginia Woolf appears as Clio, the Muse of History, on the half-landing, though Greta Garbo is also there as Melpomene, the Muse of Tragedy. The ones to east and west show the Labours and Pleasures of Life: a Covent Garden porter carrying a pile of baskets, a man filming a zebra, a Christmas pudding, one footballer tackling another. The Modern Virtues at the top of the stairs straight ahead include Winston Churchill as Defiance, the Russian

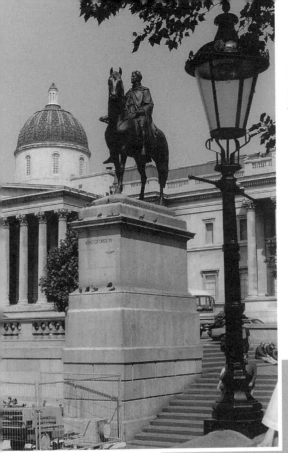

*The National
Gallery with George
IV in front*

*The Sainsbury Wing of the
National Gallery with
James II in front*

poet Anna Akhmatova as Compassion and Lord Rutherford with a splitting atom as Curiosity.

The decor of the **Central Hall** (1887), thanks, as the inscription says, to the munificence of Lord Rothschild, has been restored to its original splendour, with olive walls surmounted by a stencilled honeysuckle and Greek key frieze. Bas-relief medallions of Rubens, Titian and Raphael, and two full-length portraits by Lawrence and Sargent at their most magisterial, set the tone. The only other pictures here are four Napoleonic battlepieces by Horace Vernet – nothing too testing to start with. This is a place for decisions to be made: whether to go west for painting from c. 1510 to 1600, north for 1600 to 1700 or east for 1700 to c. 1920.

It would be jejune to suggest here what should be seen, but for some of the grandest schemes of decoration go east, to the right, where the domed octagonal **Room 36** and the rooms leading off it have recently been restored to glory, with oxblood damask walls setting off the paired green marble columns and paired gryphons. The pictures here are some of the best from eighteenth-century Venice: Canaletto and G-B. Tiepolo. Beyond, the **Sackler Room, 34**, is also splendiferously redecorated, and houses the British top-ten: Gainsborough's 'Morning Walk' and 'Watering Place'; Wright's 'Experiment on a Bird with an Air-Pump'; Turner's 'Calais Pier', 'Bridgewater Seapiece', 'Fighting Téméraire', and 'Rain, Steam and Speed'; Constable's 'Hay Wain' and 'Cornfield'. If you want to go back in time, pass through the huge **Room 32** (Guido Reni, Guercino, Caravaggio), divert north to the small **Room 16** for Vermeer and de Hooch, then to **Room 19** for Claude and **Room 20** for Poussin, before pausing among the Titians and Veroneses in the **Wohl Room, 9**.

This room also acts as entry to the bridge across to the **Sainsbury Wing**. As its name implies we owe it to the supermarket family, a consoling thought sometimes as one queues at the checkout. Earlier schemes for the site, such as the 1984 one labelled a 'monstrous carbuncle' by Prince Charles, had been bedevilled by the need to include a commercial element in the building to help meet the costs, but the Sainsburys' generosity allowed the American architect Robert Venturi to build the wing with only art in mind. That said, he also at moments had tongue in cheek, as he picked up and played with the theme of Trafalgar Square's omnipresent columns. He clustered them together, then spaced them, then allowed them to peter out, only to revive them round the corner in the form of coloured lotus-headed Egyptian ones. His touch seems to have deserted him at the back of the wing where, apart from an inscription giving some rather redundant information about earlier occupants of the site, you are confronted by expanses of largely unrelieved wall, about as dull as the earlier 1970s Orange Street extension to the Gallery nearby.

Once inside, the first impression is somewhat marred by the low ceiling, no doubt necessary to squeeze in the restaurant, etc., on the mezzanine. A generous staircase down to the special exhibition rooms in the basement could do without its giant mannered lengths of low-slung cornice or dado rail. However, the equally generous staircase going up, with its glass wall one side and incantatory list of great painters' names cut in stone on the other, raises the spirit as well as the body, in spite of the bogus iron arches overhead.

The true test of any gallery building is how well it sets off the pictures hung in it, and on this score the wing is a resounding success, increasing manyfold the impact of its Quattrocento and Northern Renaissance paintings. Apart from the portraits, this is largely sacred art, best left to speak for itself with the minimum of interference. The only problem seems to be the grease and dirt that is accumulating from passing hands on the grey semi-engaged columns that flank the arches leading from one room to another. Any fractious children can be sent, with a consenting adult, to the **micro gallery** to extract all manner of information about the collection by touching the computer screens. It is next to the **restaurant** with its wall painting, 'Crivelli's Garden', by Paula Rego. This claims to be filled with mythological heroines and saints, but the abiding impression is of a series of strong-featured black-clad women.

It would be unwise to visit the **National Portrait Gallery** immediately after the National Gallery, but it is attached to its north-east end and so logically should be discussed at this point. Once you have turned the eastern corner of the National Gallery, you will see above you a seated statue of Minerva by John Flaxman, executed in that mysterious artificial material, Coade Stone. Like her neighbour, George IV, she was originally intended for

Marble Arch, where she would have featured as Britannia. The
NPG collection, the criterion for inclusion in which is the histori-
cal significance of the sitter rather than the artistic merit of the
painting, sculpture or photograph, was begun in 1856, but it did
not get a permanent home here until 1896. Simple pleasure was
not listed as among its aims; rather it was meant to be an incentive
to 'mental exertion, to noble actions, to good conduct'. The building was paid for by a philanthropist called William Henry Alexan-
der, who owned a tidy slice of London around Thurloe Square and
who deserves to be mentioned in the same breath as the Sainsburys. Its style is called 'Italian Renaissance', though inside it has
more the aura of a Baronial Hall, with round 'Norman' arches,
coffered painted ceiling, a medieval-type chandelier and stencilled
curtains on the wall. Outside there is the usual line-up of the
famous that the Victorians could seldom resist; here it takes the
form of medallion sculptures of great historians and portraitists –
Carlyle, Macaulay, Lely, Kneller and so on.

   Take the lift from level one, noticing its doors carefully
'tromped' to simulate wood, and emerge at level five, where you
can look through an arch on to casts of royal tomb effigies from
Westminster Abbey, including that of Queen Eleanor of the
crosses. The galleries that follow in chronological order have wall
coverings suitable to their periods: wooden planking for the
earlier Tudors, stencilled hangings for the Elizabethans, panelling
for the early eighteenth century. Many of the personages already
mentioned in this book are assembled here. Nell Gwynn, Lord
Rochester crowning a monkey with bays, Samuel Pepys and a bust
of his thyroid-eyed wife are all close together. There is a lively bust
of Hogarth by Roubiliac and masterly ones of Pitt and Fox by
Nollekens; Barry's self-portrait and another by him of Dr Johnson
make one regret he spent so long on the decorations at the RSA.
Among the large group of portraits of distinguished Victorians by
G. F. Watts there is a stunner of his child-bride Ellen Terry, only
matched by J. Bastien-Lepage's picture of Henry Irving.

   St Martin's Place outside the NPG is dominated by the monument to **Edith Cavell**. The actual statue of her by Sir George
Frampton passes muster but the stone cenotaph surmounted by a
mother and child and a cross is awful. Cavell was a British nurse in

Belgium shot by the Germans in October 1915 for aiding the escape of British and French soldiers. She considered the verdict passed on her to be just. Her famous last words, 'Patriotism is not enough', were not allowed to be added to the other invocations on the memorial until some time after the war, and even then there were protests. The building behind it to the east, which houses a large Post Office, is one of the best in London from the architecturally bleak days of the 1950s and 60s.

The statue of **Sir Henry Irving** by Thomas Brock at the entrance to **Orange Street**, unlike the Lepage portrait just mentioned, conveys none of the electricity of the man. Beyond it is what looks like a small glassed-in bandstand, the entrance to the recently-excavated subterranean office of a new newspaper-with-a-difference, the *Daily Loonylugs*. Brainchild of eccentric millionaire Tony Samuelson, its gimmick is that each issue incorporates a paper hat. Some way down Orange Street, past the back entrance to the National Gallery, the Westminster Reference Library occupies the site of what was Sir Isaac Newton's town house from 1710 to 1727, which later that century became the home of the musicologist Dr Burney and his daughter Fanny, the diarist and novelist. Orange Street is meant to have been the location of the original of Dickens' *Old Curiosity Shop*. Beyond the junction with Whitcomb Street there used to be Charles II's royal tennis court, which is why the pub on the corner is called The Hand and Racquet. The Latin motto on the sign, 'Orbes orbem semper spectant', translates as 'Keep your eye on the ball'.

Go a short way, north, up Whitcomb Street and then turn right into **LEICESTER SQUARE**, since the middle of the last century a magnet for those seeking entertainment. In 1631 the Earl of Leicester got permission to build a mansion on what is now the north side of the square, on condition that the fields in front were made into a public garden. In 1656 the earl's son, Algernon Sidney, put on a play at Leicester House, probably the first in what became the heart of theatreland. The play is said to have been *Julius Caesar*, selected by Sidney as an implied criticism of Cromwell's dictatorship. Sidney, however, was no royalist but rather an ardent republican. His elder brother wrote to their father that the house 'had been better used to do a seasonable courtesy to My Lord Protector [Cromwell], than to have such a play acted in it of public affront to him, which doth much entertayne the towne.' When the earl died in 1677 the family fell out over the inheritance and the result was that the Sidneys never benefited from the 'development potential' of this part of London.

In 1717 the future George II quarrelled with his father and established a rival court at Leicester House, rented from the Sidneys, until he succeeded to the throne in 1727. In 1742 the pattern was exactly repeated by his own son Frederick, until 1751 when he died after being hit in the throat by a cricket ball:

> Here lies Fred
> Who was alive and is dead.
> Had it been his father,
> I had much rather . . .

There was a moment when it seemed that this Prince of Wales might also marry a Lady Diana Spencer, but in the end she became the wife of Topham Beauclerk (p. 42)

In those days Leicester Fields, according to J. T. Smith, 'from the rough and broken state of its ground, and the shadow of a lofty row of elms, which then stood in the road in front of most of the houses on the eastern side, was rendered a very dangerous part to pass, particularly before the streets were paved or publicly lighted.' Certainly in 1757 a Mrs King, a householder there, was murdered by her lodger who then tried to burn her remains. William Hickey reminisced:

One of the most severe floggings I received was for going . . . to gratify an idle curiosity in staring at the house in Leicester Fields . . . For many weeks after the discovery of the murder a large mob assembled in front of the house, every person in turn putting their noses to the keyhole of the front door when each individual went away perfectly satisfied that they smelt the burning of the flesh and bones.

In 1761 Joshua Reynolds moved from Great Newport Street to the western side, where he lived until his death in 1792. He could well afford the rent of £110 a year because by 1762 his annual income was £6000. He just overlapped with William Hogarth, who lived on the eastern side until he died in 1764. In 1791 Leicester House was demolished and the square declined until it was opened up to through traffic by the new Coventry Street and enlargement of Cranbourn Street in 1843. Private residences gave way to shops, exhibitions, oyster bars and Turkish baths. In 1851 Wyld's Monster Globe was erected in the middle, to cash in on visitors drawn to London by the Great Exhibition of that year in Hyde Park. It was demolished in 1862. The Moorish Panopticon building opened on the east side in 1854, but the earnestness of its exhibitions stopped it being a success until it was converted into the Alhambra Palace in 1858. This was first a circus, famous for Leotard, the original Daring Young Man on the Flying Trapeze, and Blondin, the tightrope walker; then a music hall. It even housed the Ballet Russe in 1919 and 1921 before it was finally bulldozed in 1936 and replaced by the Art Deco Odeon cinema.

Let's start at the top right corner with the **Warner Cinema**, an Art Deco gem (1938)with its decoration of figures in triple outline, on the site of Daly's, a famous Victorian music hall. On the east side, is it conceivable that number 22, Bella Pasta, next to the Odeon, is an eighteenth-century survivor? As you pass the entrance to **Irving Street**, look for number 20, inventive Italian Gothic, and once the premises of the Leicester Gallery where Monet, Renoir, Cezanne and Henry Moore had their first one-man shows in England earlier in the century. The south side of the square has the Hampshire Hotel, actually the old Royal Dental Hospital with added burgundy awnings, bay trees and fake ivy fringe, and another Odeon cinema. Cannot it be persuaded to do without its huge hoardings, which look as though they are hiding an amusing 1930s frontage?

Enter the garden at this point, by the new half-price theatre ticket booth. A lot of money and effort has gone into sprucing it up and it is just a pity that its sculptural population is so run down. It originally had a gilded lead statue of George I, erected by Prince Frederick in 1748 because he knew it would annoy his father. A hundred years later this was very decrepit and much abused by revellers. In the 1870s 'Baron' Albert Grant, an MP and newspaper proprietor, paid for the square to be properly planted and laid out, and replaced George I with a copy of Scheemakers' statue of Shakespeare in Poets' Corner at Westminster Abbey. He also

Queen's House and the Empire, Leicester Square

The mini-bandstand at the junction of Irving Street and Charing Cross Road

installed four busts of eighteenth-century figures who had lived in
or near the square: Newton, Reynolds, Hogarth and John Hunter
the surgeon. Grant, born Gottheim in Dublin, then went bank-
rupt – altogether a very Maxwellian figure.

> Honours a King can give, honour he can't:
> And Grant without honour is a Baron Grant.

Robert Louis Stevenson and his wife wrote a story called 'The
Dynamiter' about an incompetent anarchist's failed attempt to
blow up Shakespeare. It would be a kindness to try again, and
spare his head from further fouling by pigeons. The four busts,
although patched and eroded beyond recognition, have been
given elaborate new plinths. It would have been better to spend
the money on getting new ones carved; a copy of the one of Hogarth by Roubiliac in the NPG, for example. The last straw is the
thoroughly unconvincing statue of Charlie Chaplin that has joined
this motley bunch.

The north-west corner of the square is closed off by the 1960s
Swiss Centre, chocolate-coloured of course, the bells of its caril-
lon clock struck by animated peasant figures. The Empire Cinema
is on the site of the music hall of the same name owned by the
Frenchman Daniel Nicols, who ran the Café Royal. In the 1890s, a
young Sandhurst cadet called Winston Churchill made perhaps
his first public speech here. The excuse was a good-natured riot in
which some canvas screens, erected to separate the promenade
at the back of the auditorium from various bars off it, were
destroyed. The promenade was a haunt of the better class of pros-
titute and a pressure group mounting a purity campaign against
them had demanded the screens. As always, Churchill was on the
side of liberty. In 1896 the first public cinema showing in Britain
took place here.

Queen's House, on the right of the Empire, topped by a startling
green lantern, was built as an hotel in 1897. Bacchus, and a nymph
playing an anachronistic violin, preside above the arch on the second floor. The terracotta former Hotel de l'Europe (1898), with
particularly good surrounds to the bull's-eye windows on the first
floor, completes the circuit of the square. Leicester Square tube,
the end of this walk, is a few yards away, along Cranbourn Street.

INDEX

Italic numbers indicate illustrations